INTO THE DEEP

The Life You Were Meant To Live Is Calling

PHIL VALDEZ

Publisher contact information: Book Writer Corner
433 Walnut Ct Pittsburgh PA 15237, USA
e-mail: info@bookwritercorner.com
https://bookwritercorner.com/
(878) 219-4793
ISBN: 978-1-960815-49-1

Endorsements

My awesome friend pastor Phil Valdez has done it again! He's written another powerfully insightful, inspiring, and wonderfully encouraging new book, titled Into the Deep! Pastor Phil masterfully guides us into an amazing journey of discovering God's purpose for our lives. The experience and wisdom he's gained in over 30 years of being in ministry coupled with tremendous biblical knowledge and a genuine loving pastoral heart makes this book so appealing and compelling. No matter what your age, stage or phase in life may be today, this book will benefit your life, family, relationships, business or ministry. Let's go Into the Deep together!

—Dr. Michael Maiden Sr. Pastor of Church for the Nations in Phoenix Az., Author, Speaker

My friend Phil has delivered a motivating and powerful tool to help you tap into the promise that's been placed on your life! This book will ignite in you a hunger to push beyond your normal and step into the life you are called to live! Phil provides amazing insight for looking at your life, connecting with your calling, and clearing out the clutter of what's holding you back. This book is for the souls who will never settle for anything less than all they can be, do, share, and give in their lifetime!

—Rex Crain Speaker, Author, and Strategist.

Into The Deep, the life you were meant to live is calling, is a great motivating book for anyone looking to go above and beyond the life they are currently living. Phil Valdez does a awesome job combining scripture with heart felt inspiration to give his readers the Godly blueprint to start making positive changes and growth in their lives.

—Gary Cablayan Speed trainer for NFL athletes and Olympic sprinters and hurdlers.

Phil Valdez has written an amazing new book the definitely speaks to all of us. He reminds us that we all have a specific calling that is constantly calling us. In this book he helps us to find our true authentic calling and shows us the benefits that will happen for us because we are willing to be obedient to the calling.

—Tim Storey - Author/Speaker

As a former suicidal drug addict that has a robust resume of failures, mistakes and a buffet of sins, Into The Deep is a great reminder and inspiration that God's not done and in spite of my past, He is inviting me into the deepest parts of His heart.

—Rodrigo Vargas//RevRod® UNION Houston

Contents

Introduction

This book is dedicated to everyone who is living in the tension between who they are now and who they are meant to be. It is for the person who has a sense that their best version is waiting to be revealed. Your calling is calling! It is time to activate your divine purpose.

God has handpicked you to live beyond your perceived limitations and what you thought was impossible. God desires for His life to dwell and flow through your being. There is nothing normal about this. You were not designed to be mediocre; therefore, refrain from aiming for average. This is an astonishing life, not one of mere existence but of significance and importance. It is the life you were created for! The life you were meant to live.

God is about to do something new in your life. It will be unprecedented. The path that God has prepared for you will surpass any expectations you have about your own life. Right now, there is no point of reference for what awaits. It is not a life that is a replica of someone else's. What He is about to do in you has never been seen in your mother, father, grandparents, or neighbors. The

Bible says,

"No eye has seen, no ear has heard and no one's heart has imagined all the things that God has prepared for those who love him."10. But God has revealed them to us through His Spirit.

For the Spirit searches all things, yes, the deep things of God.
—1 Corinthians 2:9,10 NKJV

There is an awareness in you that has arisen that causes you to think that there could be more than what is visible on the surface. There is a longing in you for something more. Shallow living does not suit you, and you know it. This is evidence that a stirring has begun inside you.

In my experience, the stirring would not go away, and it became more constant and often recurred when I least expected it to. At first, I would dismiss the thoughts as momentary ideas and feelings. Yet when they became more frequent, I realized these were more than mere thoughts. A desire was being born within me, yet somehow, I knew it did not originate with me.

As I prayed, read my Bible, and sought God, I began to understand that the desire emanated from God's calling on my life. It was indeed an invitation. The life God meant for me to live was creating a longing, a yearning, a hunger in my heart that produced a desire for a greater dimension of existence that I had yet to experience.

The Bible tells us of David, a man after God's heart, who wrote in Psalm 42 about the tension he experienced in his mind and heart. Although David's heart intensely desired to know and seek God, his mind was sometimes unsettled.

David illustrates his heart's desire by using the analogy of a deer panting for water. Water is an essential ingredient for life. A deer will seek water after being chased or hunted by predators. In the day's heat, the watering hole becomes the assemblage of many animals seeking the same relief. The deer will pant and cry for the water, knowing his survival depends on it. Drinking deeply from the water, the deer is refreshed, renewed, and full of life.

David concludes this tension between his heart and mind by describing the yearning as "Deep calling unto deep."

> *"Deep calls to deep at the noise of Your waterfalls; all Your waves and billows have gone over me."*—Psalms 42:7 NIV

The Wycliffe Bible translated it this way: "One depth calls to another depth." We must understand that for God to be able to call a deeper purposefulness out of us, it means that God has already deposited within us the very depth for those purposes to dwell. You already have a capacity within you to live at a deeper level, the level you have always wanted to live at.

God created you this way. You were created by Him and for Him. That's why nothing else can fulfill or satisfy you except for His plans and purposes for your life. Your response to His call will not only determine if what He has placed in you will be revealed, but it will also determine what level you can live at.

We may hesitate to respond to this call because, over time, we can begin to define our lives by what we've gone through. The circumstances and situations that have impacted our lives become a lid we now live under, so we cling to the stability of the shore. We have made our residence there and have determined that this is where we belong, so we never really explore the possibility of something deeper. Faith has become unnecessary because we don't venture out further than what we have previously seen or experienced.

A mindset can develop where we think we have seen and heard it all and that nothing will ever change. These are the words of someone who has settled on the shore. They are not living life to the fullest, but they are just merely existing. Their focus is on the past, not the future.

There is hope. Don't settle. There are still thoughts you have yet to think about. There are dreams and visions you have yet to see. There are places you have yet to go and things you have yet to do. Your most significant achievements have yet to be accomplished, yet God, through His Spirit, desires to reveal them to you.

The future is now upon us, so we must look ahead. It is time to leave the past on the shore behind us and step out in faith into our extraordinary God-given destiny. It is risky, but God can do more with our future than we have done with our past. Only God can truly make us the best versions of ourselves. This life is possible!

When we launch into the deep with God, we will find that He wants to show us His goodness and glory. He will surprise us. His plan will astound us and leave us in awe. To experience such a life, one must take a bold step and abandon the ease and familiarity of the shore to explore the vast depths of the ocean.

Say yes! It is the best decision you will ever make. The life you were meant to live is a calling! You were born for this!

Live deeply,

Phil Valdez

CHAPTER 1

MOVE FORWARD

Is it possible to have the worst and best day of your life all happen in the same 24 hours?

That's what happens to Simon. What if one day you woke up and the day started like any other ordinary day, and everything just seemed the same? You know that life can be mundane at times. You have the day's routine memorized, so it's easy to check out mentally and emotionally. What happens then is that you can end up sleepwalking through the day. So, you arrive at work and put in just enough effort to achieve the day's goals, but you find that you're not productive. Not only are you not productive, but you also regressed, and the day becomes a total failure. Now you're flat out exhausted and have nothing to show for it. You're now ready to quit because you've had enough. It's time to throw in the towel.

You're done!

This is exactly how Simon feels when he encounters Jesus.

1.So it was, as the multitude pressed about Him to hear the word of God, that He stood by the Lake of Gennesaret, 2. and saw two boats standing by the lake; but the fishermen had gone from them and were washing their nets. 3. Then He got into one of the boats, which was Simon's and asked him to put out a little from the land. And He sat down and taught the multitudes from the boat. 4. When He had stopped speaking, He said to Simon, "Launch out into the deep and let down your nets for a catch." 5. But Simon answered and said to Him, "Master, we have toiled all night and caught nothing; nevertheless, at Your word I will let down the net." 6. And when they had done this, they caught a great number of fish, and their net was breaking. 7. So they signaled to their partners in the other boat to come and help them. And they came and filled both the boats, so that they began to sink."

—Luke 5:1-7 NKJV

The God Who Sees

It was not uncommon for thousands of people to want to hear Jesus speak. In this case, they pressed Him to the shore of Lake Gennesaret, also known as the Sea of Galilee. Jesus saw two boats and decided that He would like to use Simon's boat. He asked Simon to push it out a little so He could continue to teach.

This boat was significant to Simon because he was a fisherman and a business owner. The boat was used to provide a service for his customers and bring Simon the income needed to sustain his livelihood, support his family, and bring the profits necessary to ensure the future of his business.

In essence, Jesus asked Simon if He could use what was significant to Simon for His purpose, The Kingdom of God. Simon allowed Jesus to do so. We must understand that whenever Jesus places a demand in our lives, He plans to set us up for an incredible supply. The miracles of Jesus often began with an instruction. The response to the instruction will determine whether you experience what Jesus has for you or not.

Often, we can question why Jesus would ask us for anything. Why would Jesus use Simon's boat? The truth is Jesus doesn't need a boat at all. He is God. He created the oceans and the seas. Jesus can walk on water, yet Jesus knew what Simon needed. Simon needed Jesus in his boat.

Jesus knew that. Just like Simon, we need Jesus in the boat of our lives, too.

Jesus didn't need Simon's boat, Simon needed Jesus In His Boat.

We must understand that when Jesus asks us to give Him what is significant and precious to us, Jesus is not trying to take something from us, but instead get something to us. This was a setup. Jesus was setting Simon up for the miracle that Simon needed. Simon didn't know this, but Jesus strategically picked his boat.

This story always blesses me because it illustrates Jesus' ability to see and love many people like the multitude, yet not miss an individual like Simon. One of God's names is El Roi. El Roi is the Hebrew name for God, meaning "The God who sees me." Even with the billions of people on the planet, God still sees and recognizes you.

Don't Make Friends with Failure

When Jesus finished teaching, He noticed Simon's situation. Simon had failed to catch any fish. He literally caught nothing, and as a result, his nets were empty. I do not doubt that Simon was a skilled professional, but this day was a total failure, or so Simon thought.

Failure can happen to the best of us. Are there areas of your life that you feel you have failed? It could be that you lost your job, or you feel like your dream has died. For others, it could be a failed relationship, whether in a marriage or with your children. You know you are not living up to your full potential. Failure has become a part of your identity, leading you to believe that failure is all you can expect in the future. It can be like a scarlet letter branding your life, yet you know this is not your true identity.

Failure can be devastating. Sometimes, unfulfilled expectations can leave you feeling lost and questioning your life's purpose. It can also lead to disappointment and discouragement. Then there appears to be a defect or void somewhere in your life that cannot be reconciled.

For Simon, a lack of fish represented a lack of success. His failure resulted in empty nets. What could empty nets mean to you? Obviously, you don't have a boat and need to cast out a net to get fish. However, I am sure that you have had certain expectations about some of the outcomes in your life, and when they didn't come to fruition, it left you feeling empty.

Failure can result in an empty bank account, making life difficult. Certain poor decisions could have been made in the context of relationships, leaving a void filled with loneliness. As a result, you may be wondering what steps you should take next. You might think, "Why move forward if there will be more of the same?"

How you respond to your failure will determine your future. Jonathan C. Maxwell said, *"The difference between average people and achieving people is their perception of and response to failure."*

We can't just stay here; we must respond. We can move forward because, with Jesus in the boat of our lives, failure is never final. Just because you failed doesn't mean you're a failure. We must refuse to let it become part of our identity and define our lives. A failure is an event that happened; it is not your identity with Jesus, so don't make friends with it.

Faith, The Antidote For Failure

Jesus didn't overlook Simon's lack of accomplishment, but He addressed it. I want you to understand Jesus' heart. He saw the empty nets, and He didn't just say, "I'm sorry, Simon, goodbye and take care. I'm going to heal a guy with leprosy. That's more important." Jesus wanted to help and be involved.

Do you know what I love about this? Jesus addresses where Simon is because He wants to intervene. Jesus wants to do the same for you. What was important to Simon was important to Jesus; for Simon, it was the fish and his business. What's important and valuable to you is valuable to God.

As we learn to launch into the deep, we must note that Jesus met Simon on the shore. In the middle of his failure, Jesus met Simon right where he was. Before Jesus would take Simon deeper, Jesus had to meet Simon where he was.

We all start somewhere. Initially, it's on the beach of life, and then slowly, we enter the shallow water before progressing into the deep. Jesus desires to be part of every stage in our life and development. Jesus' intention wasn't to leave Simon in the shallow with empty nets, so He gave him an instruction. Jesus already had the solution for Simon. Think about this for a moment: Jesus knew where the fish were and already had them waiting for Simon. Jesus already has the perfect solution for you, too. This is so exciting; I wonder what Jesus has waiting for you in the deep. Jesus spoke the exact words Simon needed to hear when Simon needed it.

Jesus said, *"Launch into the deep and let down your nets."* In other words, move forward! That's the answer: don't stay where you are in the shallow; no, go deeper!

Jesus spoke faith directly into Simon's failure. Jesus' words are always pregnant and charged with faith and life. Faith is vital in our relationship with God. The writer of Hebrews writes,

> *But without faith, it is impossible to please him: for he that cometh to God must believe that he is, and that he is a rewarder of them that diligently seek him".* —Hebrews 11:6 KJV

Jesus spoke faith directly into Simon's failure.

Why would Jesus want Simon to have faith to move forward? Faith activates God's miraculous power. Faith is essential to access your future. Your future is ahead of you, not behind you. We must stop living in the past and allowing ourselves to be chained to past events. It is unnecessary to live in the past; because, we get stuck and then remain the same.

Jesus loved Simon and wanted more for him. Jesus wanted more for Simon than Simon wanted for himself. Love is an essential ingredient to faith. Faith works by love. Faith is easy when you know God wants what is best for you and loves you. You can move forward!

Faith came to Simon through Jesus' very words. Faith comes to us when we hear God's word, so we have what we need to please God and see Him work in our lives.

So then faith comes by hearing, and hearing by the word of God. —Romans 10:17 KJV

Now faith is the substance of things hoped for, the evidence of things not seen. —Hebrews 11:1 KJV.

Notice the scripture says, "Now faith is." This means that faith must start right now, no matter what the circumstance is or looks like. In the middle of your current situation, faith must begin at this very moment because it becomes the foundation to move forward. When we trust with an expectation that what we haven't seen yet will be visible because Jesus said it, then we will experience the miraculous.

The very essence of faith is that faith believes before it sees, yet if you believe in faith, you will see. Faith brings the unseen into reality. The Message translation says it this way.

> *The fundamental fact of existence is that this trust in God, this faith, is the firm foundation under everything that makes life worth living. It's our handle on what we can't see.*
>
> —Hebrews 11:1 MSG

Our faith and trust in Jesus become a firm foundation in deep waters. Jesus was telling Simon to move forward from his failure. We must do the same. The way we do this is to stop focusing on our failure and look to Jesus and what He said. Although the future is always unknown, we must look to the One who knows the future. God's word is always sure and the anchor for living in the deep. Yes, I am in the deep, yet God's word anchors me, so I am secure. The great news is that we don't move forward alone; we move forward with the revelation that Jesus is with us. That's what makes the difference.

But let's be honest; it's a little hard to move forward sometimes. Why? Often, everything we see is from the past. Take out your phone and look at Instagram; your pictures are from the past, right? You look at your videos; they are moments captured from the past.

When you walk into your house today, you will see the pictures of your family on the wall, all from moments of the past. So, we're constantly reminded of the past by what we see. Therefore, we must believe beyond what we see.

Now, for some of us, our past was great. We've had incredible victories. One of the areas that keep some people from moving forward and experiencing a deeper life is past victories. They don't realize God wants to take them from strength to strength, and victory to victory, so they settle. They exist, but they are not fully alive anymore. They have seen some dreams come true, yet God wants us to dream again. It's tough to move forward when staring into the rearview mirror.

Therefore, your focus is imperative to moving forward. Failure will cause you to be past-possessed, while faith is always future-focused with high expectations. Failure will try to rob you of your faith by wanting you to rehearse your past constantly. Your past doesn't have to be a prison that keeps you stuck. Your past is not your prophecy or the forecast for your future.

Failure will cause you to be past possessed, while faith is always future-focused.

So, if you are feeling like Simon or like you have failed, I encourage you to listen to Jesus' words. He tells you,

"Launch out into the deep and let down your nets." He is saying to you, "Have faith." And if you do, I believe you will see the miraculous like Simon saw. A whole new future.

The good news is that God does not consult our past to give us the future He has for us. Jesus must be the focus of our faith because our future is in Him. Faith looks to Jesus!

Looking unto Jesus the author and finisher of our faith
—Hebrews 12:2 KJV

The Amplified and the Amplified Classic Bible translation helps us to understand how faith works,

[Looking away from all that will distract us and] focusing our eyes on Jesus, who is the Author and Perfecter of faith [the first incentive for our belief and the One who brings our faith to maturity]—Hebrews 12:2. AMP

The Amplified Classic adds:

[Bringing it to maturity and perfection] —Hebrews 12:2.

So, it's Jesus who always brings my faith to perfection. This isn't a faith in your faith. So many people are trying to determine the size of their faith. They don't move forward because they think their faith isn't big or strong enough. No matter what size you think your faith is, look to Jesus. JESUS MAKES YOUR FAITH PERFECT! He is the perfecter of our faith!

What Moving Forward Means

Simon understood what moving forward would mean. He weighed the options in his head. Launching out again would mean getting up and going out again. The nets he just cleaned would get dirty again. It would take more time and effort, and the results could be the same. Is it really worth it?

Nobody would want to relive the experience and have the same emotions again. We think, "I can't afford another failure and have more of the same." Have you ever felt this way? For us, moving forward would mean getting up and trying again, living, loving, giving, and forgiving again.

Simon's initial response to Jesus was to say what he felt. He said, "I have toiled all night and caught nothing." The word "toil" in the Greek language means "being worn out, tired, and faint to the point of exhaustion."

Simon's first response was the result of his own work and self-effort. He did everything he knew to do and still had no results. This can happen when we are trying to live just by our strength.

However, Simon made a remarkable decision. He chose faith over his feelings. Faith is not just a mere belief. It's not faith until there is a corresponding action.

Faith illustrates what it believes by the action it produces. Simon said, "Nevertheless, at your word, Jesus, I will let down the nets."

Simon chose faith over his feelings.

The word, "word" in Greek means a "rhema word." When we read the written Word of God, it is called "logos" in Greek. A rhema word is a "right now" word that God will speak to you, giving you a sense of direction and knowledge. A rhema word is perfect for your current situation, telling you what to do next.

There is tension here because Simon's fishing expertise conflicts with Jesus' words. Simon is a professional and knows that some of the best fishing happens at night, not during the day. It would have been easy for Simon to look at Jesus and respond, "I'm the fisherman; you're the teacher. What do you know about fishing?"

But what does Jesus know about fish? That is a great question. The answer is that He knows everything about them because fish were His idea in the first place. He created them. Jesus knew more about fish than Simon did.

I can only imagine what Simon was thinking: launching out deeper when there was no previous success. This seems absurd, yet Simon did what seemed absurd.

Operating in faith will often defy human logic and prior experiences.

Empty To Overflow

Jesus led Simon to go deeper; when Simon launched out this time, he was not alone. The results were nothing like he had ever seen before in his career; it was unfathomable. There were fish everywhere! His nets were so filled that they began to break. The boat started to sink. It was a net-breaking, boat-sinking catch. What a miracle!

This shows us that God doesn't just want to fix us or the problem, but He wants to fill us. He wants our lives to be overflowing. When Jesus instructed Simon on what to do, Simon wasn't responsible for the results; Simon was responsible for responding. Jesus would bring about the results. Simon could not control the outcomes, but he could control his obedience to Jesus' instruction.

Simon's experience reminds me of a story I read once in a First Post article that encouraged me. It was a real life phenomenon that happened when fish fell from the sky.

It was said that Manuel de Jesús Subirana, a Catholic missionary from Spain who lived in the 1800s, prayed and asked God to help ease the region's hunger and poverty in Yoro, Honduras, where he lived.

Soon after he issued his plea, the legend goes, it began to rain fish. Literally, fish were falling out of the sky. Food for everyone! The provision came. The fish did not really "rain" in the sense of condensing out of water vapor.

The fish that fell from the sky used to be in the sea. How did they reach the skies? One explanation is that when powerful air disturbances travel over bodies of water, they can form waterspouts. These waterspouts can then pull up water, as well as any fish that happen to be swimming in the area. The air lifts the water and fish up into the air. When the strong wind loses its energy, the fish fall.

The residents of Yoro call this yearly incident Lluvia de Peces (lit. "rain of fish"). Most locals attribute the occurrence to the prayers of Manuel. It's so important that we don't limit God! He can do the miraculous! Empty nets are not the end. Jesus has the fish ready! Let it rain, fish!

Simon's encounter with Jesus shows us that miraculous results can come out of our greatest failure. See, problems in our lives are just opportunities to experience God's power. Personally, I don't use the word "problem" anymore. I like to use the word "opportunity." You may say, "I have many problems." No, you have many opportunities to see God work in your life. And that's exciting! The word "problem" is associated with feelings of tension and negativity, while the word "opportunity" brings about expectation and excitement with it. I'm excited to see what God will do. There's so much more in store for you! Therefore, you can't quit; we must launch out deeper.

Look at the impact Simon's obedience had: This miracle not only changed his life, but it impacted the lives of all those connected to him. He had to call in his partners. His partners experienced the miraculous because Simon decided to launch out. This is another reason why your future is so vital. Many will be impacted and inspired by what God did for you. I always say someone is waiting on the other side of your obedience. Until one day, when we step into Heaven, we may never truly know just how many people will be affected by our obedience.

Because Simon obeyed, we are reading about his life today. Notice that God didn't give Simon just enough to make ends meet. God wanted Simon to experience an undeniably supernatural overflow beyond Simon's own ability. For this to happen, Jesus had to call Simon out of his own depth of understanding, logic, and strength.

Jesus had to call Simon out of his own depth of understanding, logic, and strength.

Simon was in the perfect place to see a demonstration of Jesus' power. Don't underestimate what God can do.

Jesus can take an empty life and fill it to overflow with His presence, power, provision, peace, and joy.

Jesus wanted to show Simon what He could do through him. And just like that, God accelerated Simon's life. Acceleration happens in the deep. Simon went from empty to overflow. God is about to accelerate your life.

When we choose to venture out into the deep with God and prioritize faith over failures and feelings, God can turn the worst day of our lives into one of the best days of our lives. Get ready; overflow is in your future. Move forward! It's worth it!

CHAPTER 2

DEFINING THE DEEP

What is "the deep"? That's a good question since this is where Jesus instructed Simon to launch. Can we really define what "deep" means? We can, and we should. I wonder what your definition of "the deep" would be.

People use the word "deep" in different contexts. Traditionally, this term is used to measure the distance farthest away from the shore. Someone else may use the word "deep" to describe something they didn't fully understand. It was beyond them.

For example, someone may ask what the pastor talked about on Sunday. The person who heard the message might respond, "I don't know, but wow, it was deep!" This implies it was something so vast that it's indescribable and not quantifiable.

When Jesus instructed Simon in Luke 5:4 to "Launch out into the deep and let down your nets for a catch," was He talking about the depth of the water, or was there a more profounder meaning behind His words? Could it have meant more? With Jesus, there's always more.

I've learned to look up words in the Bible in the original language because it's more expansive and shows the original meaning and intent. The New Testament is translated from Greek to English. I thought looking up the word "deep" to learn what Jesus was saying would be essential.

In the "Complete Word Study Dictionary," a Greek English dictionary edited by Spiros Zodhiates, the word "deep" is "bathos" in Greek.

"Deep" in the Greek language means depth, metaphorically greatness, profoundness — *"the secret unrevealed purposes of God."*

The Secret, Unrevealed Purposes Of God

Wow! This definition literally blew me away. It adds a greater dimension to Simon's encounter with Jesus than just catching fish. As Simon contemplated his unsuccessful endeavors, his trade, and catching fish, Jesus had a greater plan for his life that He was eager to reveal. Jesus had already mapped out a glorious destiny for Simon that had yet to unfold. Simon had no idea, just like we don't at times.

Jesus saw more in Simon than just a successful businessman. Jesus saw more in Simon than Simon saw in himself. All Simon heard was an instruction to "Launch out into the deep," which really didn't make sense at the time. Let me rephrase what Jesus said to Simon in the Greek language translation: "Simon, launch out into the secret purposes I have already prepared for you, which I will reveal."

We may think this only applies to Simon, but in the book of Ecclesiastes, King Solomon writes that there is a sense of divine purpose that God has placed in every human heart that has yet to be revealed. King Solomon calls it eternity. Eternity is in the heart of every person. We were created with eternity in us. What a captivating truth!

He has made everything beautiful and appropriate in its time. He has also planted eternity [a sense of divine purpose] in the human heart [a mysterious longing which nothing under the sun can satisfy, except God]—yet man cannot find out (comprehend, grasp*) what God has done (His overall plan) from the beginning to the end.* —Ecclesiastes 3:11 AMP

The Amplified Classic describes it this way:

[A divinely implanted sense of a purpose working through the ages which nothing under the sun but God alone can satisfy]
—Ecclesiastes 3:11 AMP CLASSIC

Take a moment and think about eternity. What a thought! I'd like to know what your current situation looks like, in the light of eternity. The idea of eternity takes your eyes off the moment to focus on something bigger and grander than yourself.

I'm not trying to make light of what you are facing; however, it is crucial to acknowledge that there exists a greater objective in motion and a wider perspective that needs to be considered. God knows this, so He intentionally speaks to you where you are to move you where He knows you should be.

He created you on purpose with a destiny to fulfill. King Solomon writes that we could never comprehend our beginning and what our end could be without God. He is the only one who can satisfy this mysterious longing that our human heart has. He will make sense of it all.

As you will discover later as you read, what Jesus had planned for Simon was beyond Simon's wildest dreams and ambitions! Compared to Jesus' plans, Simon's goals and projections for the next five years would be insignificant. If Simon thought his whole purpose and goal for his life was to be a successful business owner and have a thriving fishing business, Simon would have thought to small.

Simon would have lived a frustrated life, constantly feeling like there was more to it, and indeed, there was. Simon's influence on humanity would have been minimal at best. It is essential to consider that Simon's life would not have had an eternal impact should he have chosen not to respond to Jesus' instruction.

God's purpose for your life originates in God, who is eternal. Therefore, the purpose of your life will impact the eternal realm. Thus, God has set eternity in your heart because He is Eternal. This means the purpose which God has for you will live beyond you.

The purpose which God has for you will live beyond you.

Eternity in the original language also means an unending future, perpetual, yet concealed. Simon's purpose would not only affect generations to come but would have an eternal impact, which we will explore in an upcoming chapter.

God still has purposes already planned for your life that are a secret to you only because they have not been revealed yet. God is calling and inviting you to enter them so they may be unveiled. This is the life you were meant to live.

God is initiating an encounter with you today, just like Jesus started getting into Simon's boat strategically. Jesus wants to be received into your life. Every part of your life. We can call on Him because the answer is available even though you don't know it or see it. Just like the fish were waiting on Peter, God's solution is ready for you to step into.

Thus says the Lord Who made [the earth], the Lord Who formed it to establish it—the Lord is His name: 3Call to Me and I will answer you and show you great and mighty things, fenced-in and hidden, which you do not know (do not distinguish and recognize, have knowledge of and understand).
—Jeremiah 33:2-3 AMPC

God has great and mighty things in store for your life! The magnitude of it will fascinate you!

Awakening The Wonder

For many, the thought of deep waters can trigger a fear of drowning. I understand. I had to be rescued by a lifeguard during a scuba diving lesson at a water park when I was thirteen. We were swimming in the pool's deep end, and I got tired. I could no longer move my body because of the exhaustion. The lifeguards pulled me to the shore on the artificial beach, and then they gave me CPR. My first impression of the pool's deep end was a near-death experience.

Learning how to navigate in the deep was necessary because, just like during my scuba class, life is full of uncertainties that require us to be prepared. I was getting ready to enjoy a day at the water park when something unexpected occurred—an overwhelming situation for which I was not prepared.

Here's the good news. Whether you choose to explore the deep waters like Simon at Jesus' invitation or you were thrust into the deep due to life's unexpected circumstances, the principles, and truths for navigating deep waters remain the same. Why was it that God called Simon into deep waters? What is it about the deep?

It's in the deep where God does His best work.

The scriptures assure us that it's in the deep where God does His best work in us. Let this scripture be an anchor to you as you navigate:

> *They that go down to the sea in ships, that do business in great waters; 24 These see the works of the Lord, and His wonders in the deep.* —Psalm 107:23,24 KJV.

The Passion Translation says that we will witness His power and experience His breathtaking wonders:

> *We were witnesses of God's power out in the ocean deep; we saw breathtaking wonders upon the high seas.*
> —Psalm 107:24 TPT

Do you want to live a small and shallow life? I don't want to stay in a little pond while there are great waters to explore. I want to do business in great waters, that's where

I want to live. How about you? I want to experience God's breathtaking wonders. This only happens in the deep.

Let this encourage you. God's best work is done in the deep because it requires the most faith. It's the place where God can empty us from ourselves, and all the temporary support systems that we have relied on are exposed. In the deep, we must release our grip and control and rely on God entirely with complete trust.

God's invitation to join Him in the deep is not to watch you drown. He intends to awaken the wonder in your life and take you beyond yourself so He can reveal everything unknown about your life and future.

CHAPTER 3

FINDING YOUR FUTURE

According to an article by the American Psychological Association, 76% of individuals in the United States experience stress due to concerns about future events. Could this be the reason why over 70 million people read horoscopes daily for insight? Would you be honest enough to say that at one time or another, you got a little excited about opening a fortune cookie, hoping to find some words of wisdom to inspire you about what was to come next?

Once, I sat beside a man in a restaurant who opened his fortune cookie and found nothing inside. His face turned white. Does this mean that there is no future for him? Well, it was probably just a human error. Someone probably should have put the piece of paper in the cookie that day, they didn't realize someone's futures was depending on it. All kidding aside, what does it mean? I imagine that is what he was thinking. It means we should stop relying on fortune cookies or horoscopes to help us find our future. They will mislead us. God does not inspire any of those things, which can all be tainted by human error.

God Knows The Future

Although life can be unpredictable and the future is unknown, it brings comfort to know that God is already present in the future and aware of what is to come. Jesus said,

> *I am the Alpha and the Omega, the First and the Last, the Beginning and the End.* —Revelation 22:13 KJV.

Not only was God in the beginning before we were created, but Jesus also said, "I AM the beginning and the end."

In Jesus is the beginning and the end at the same time. It's not one or the other; it's both simultaneously. Our mind cannot conceive this, yet we must believe it by faith. All our beginnings and endings are found in Him. You may feel like one season of your life is ending, but God is not finished with you yet. He is right there with a new beginning for you. He will give you the new beginning you need to have the ending He has desired for you.

With God, every ending is already infused with a new beginning. Faith is not only the antidote for failure, it is the key ingredient in accessing the future God has planned for us. This is what Jesus desired for Simon all along. He wanted Simon to experience a new beginning—a whole new life. As Simon reflected on the lack of fish, Jesus was focused on Simon's extravagant future.

With God, every ending is already infused with a new beginning.

How did Jesus go about giving Simon a whole new life? Jesus showed Simon His goodness. Jesus demonstrated to Simon that He could make the impossible, possible. Jesus gave Simon the best catch of his life.

Let's examine how Peter's life was impacted.

When Simon Peter saw it, he fell down at Jesus' knees, saying, "Depart from me, for I am a sinful man, O Lord!" 9 For he and all who were with him were astonished at the catch of fish which they had taken; 10. and so also were James and John, the sons of Zebedee, who were partners with Simon.
—Luke 5:8-10 NKJV.

Simon was astonished, filled with amazement at what Jesus had done! You will be, too. An encounter with Jesus changed the trajectory of Simon's life. My friends, only Jesus can take a man who was worn out and tired to the point of exhaustion from working all night and fill him with amazement.

Simon's story shows us that when we come to Jesus, we come just as we are. No matter the failure or the sin, by turning to Jesus, He can bring about actual new life transformation. We don't have to be perfect before we come to Him; we don't have to have it all together. Jesus invites us to just come.

Come to Me, all you who labor and are heavy-laden and overburdened, and I will cause you to rest. [I will ease and relieve and refresh your souls.] 29 Take My yoke upon you and learn of Me, for I am gentle (meek) and humble (lowly) in heart, and you will find rest] relief and ease and refreshment and recreation and blessed quiet) for your souls. 30 For My yoke is wholesome (useful, sound—not harsh, brutal, sharp, or pressing, but comfortable, gracious, and pleasant), and My burden is light and easy to be borne. —Matthew 11:28-30 AMPC

The Message translation says it beautifully as well.

"Are you tired? Worn out and burned out on religion? Come to me. Get away with me, and you'll recover your life. I'll show you how to take a real rest. Walk with me and work with me—watch how I do it. Learn the unforced rhythms of grace. I won't lay anything heavy or ill-fitting on you. Keep company with me, and you'll learn to live freely and lightly."
—Matthew 11:28-30 MSG.

In Jesus' day, farmers used a yoke; it looked like a collar that laid behind their neck and on their shoulders. The yoke was to bond two oxen to each other. The farmers used the yoke to train young oxen to plow the fields by partnering them with more substantial and more mature oxen. The job of the younger ox was to follow in the same direction and keep pace with the teacher ox. The older ox pulled most of the weight and understood the commands of the plow driver.

If the young ox followed the older ox, everything was fine. But the work became much more difficult when the younger ox decided to speed up or fall behind. Only by keeping pace with the older ox could the younger ox complete the day's work without collapsing from exhaustion.

When we are yoked to Jesus Christ, He sets the pace that we need to accomplish the future that He has planned and carries most of the weight. His yoke is a different kind of yoke, one that is perfectly fitted to assist and benefit us in fulfilling His purpose. We must be yoked with Jesus to allow Him to set the pace because our future can only be found in Him. It doesn't mean that there won't be challenges; however, when we begin to lose rhythm and exhaustion sets in, Jesus' very own strength permeates us to go the distance because we are yoked to Him.

Mind-Sets Matter

Your mindset is how your mind is set. Your perspective is how you process things. It's your point of view. What is your mind set on today? Do you have a mindset that things will never change, and life will never improve? Or do you believe that all things are possible with God? God loves to show us that He has a better life designed for us than we could plan for ourselves.

Simon responds to Jesus by falling to his knees and acknowledging that he is unworthy. Simon knew he was a sinful man. When Simon experiences the goodness and glory of Jesus, this causes him to repent. Look for God's goodness in your life! The scripture says that repentance is the proper response to God's goodness.

God's kindness is intended to lead you to repent (to change your mind and inner man to accept God's will).
—Romans 2:4, AMPC

The word "repent" in the original language means a change of mind, as it appears to one who repents of a purpose he has formed or of something he has done. To change one's mind for the better, heartily to amend with abhorrence of one's past sins. Repentance is a change of mind that produces a change of heart.

Many people have given up on living a deeper life because they believe they don't deserve a miraculous future because of their sins. Their minds are set on this. Sin will always cause you to settle. The truth is Simon didn't deserve it either, yet Jesus, by His grace, gave Simon what he didn't deserve. This is what grace is.

In my *book "The Power of Thank You – The Key to Finding Joy Again,"* I thoroughly define God's grace. The Greek word for grace is "charis." Grace (charis), in the Greek language, means a benefit. It's God's unearned, undeserved, unmerited favor in our lives. Grace also indicates gratification, acceptance, and kindness granted or desired.

When you experience God's grace, faith arises. Faith is the correct response to God's grace. Faith is the receiver and receives what grace gives. This is the anatomy of a miracle. All miracles flow from God's grace, yet to receive His extraordinary grace, we must believe in faith that it is possible.

Simon acknowledged his sin, and he repented. We should do the same. Forgiveness has been given to all by Jesus because of His great sacrifice on the cross, yet we must receive it by faith to experience it. It's not enough to know that God forgives. We must be active in receiving it no matter what we have done or no matter how many times we've done it.

It would have been easy for Simon to focus on all his sins and believe that Jesus didn't want to forgive him or couldn't forgive him. The truth is, for us, what Jesus did on the cross is more remarkable than whatever you have ever done or what you will ever do. We must keep our focus on the finished work of Jesus Christ, not our failures. Since Jesus forgives you, then you can forgive you. Sometimes, forgiving ourselves can be challenging.

Self-hatred can set in when we feel the guilt and shame. Jesus shed His blood on the cross to cleanse us of our sins.

> 7 *But if we walk in the light as He is in the light, we have fellowship with one another, and the blood of Jesus Christ His Son cleanses us from all sin.* —1 John 1:7 NKJV

Notice that the scripture describes the blood of Jesus as active and moving. The word "cleanse" is not written in past tense. It is written as "cleanses." That means it is a constant flow cleansing our lives when we come under the blood of Jesus. The magnitude of the power of Jesus' blood is always present. This is powerful because it's not just a past event, so this is where we must place our faith and focus. When we do, we will live forgiven and free. I'm thankful for His forgiveness in my life. Moving forward in freedom is compelled by His extravagant forgiveness. By His grace, receive all the forgiveness you need today and every day!

When we read Matthew 11:28-30, did you notice how often it talks about rest, especially rest for your souls? Your soul is your mind, will, and emotions. In this definition, the original Greek language, the word "rest" means to refresh and recreate. We need a new mindset to be recreated in us.

God can create a whole new mindset in us. We need this to discover His future for us; otherwise, we will think too small. A limited perspective will lead to a limited life. This happens when we focus solely on our thoughts, self-effort, and strength.

Why does God want to show us His goodness? First, He wants to change how you see Him. The way you see God is the way you will relate to Him. When you have the correct view of God, then it helps us to have the right view of ourselves. We will learn about this in the chapters ahead.

The way you see God, is the way you will relate to Him.

You cannot enter the future with an incorrect view of God or yourself. Our mindset must change. He reveals His goodness so you can see Him as He truly is.

> *And do not be conformed to this world, but be transformed by the renewing of your mind, that you may prove what is that good and acceptable and perfect will of God.*
> — Romans 12:2, NKJV

The word "transformed" is "metamorphoō" in Greek. It's where we get the word "metamorphosis." It means to change into another form, to transform, to transfigure. It's what happens when a caterpillar changes into a butterfly.

We have two choices: to conform to the world's mindset that says, "It is what it is, so it will be what it will be," or we can allow God to transform our thinking. Therefore, reading the Bible, which is God's Word and His thoughts towards us, is so important. It changes our minds to think about how God thinks. God's word will grow and expand your thinking patterns.

God's thoughts are higher and more expansive than ours. This should bring us hope and inspire us. God wants us to know Him to the point that we think like Him, because in order to go higher we must think on a higher level.

> *"For as the heavens are higher than the earth, so are My ways higher than your ways, and My thoughts than your thoughts."*—Isaiah 55:9-10 NKJV

Look at the dimensions that Isaiah describes, as far as the heavens are from the earth, can that even be calculated? The heavens aren't just where we see the layer of clouds. That is what we would call the first heaven, then there is the second heaven where the sun, moon and stars are residing, we would call that space. Can anyone measure space? How can we measure the furthest depth of the ocean's floor on earth, to the highest point in any galaxy? There are galaxies yet to be discovered. In other words, God's thoughts have infinite possibility.

> [37] *For with God nothing is ever impossible!*
> —Luke 1:37 NKJV

God thinks creatively and with possibility. His thoughts are miraculous! His thoughts are filled with vision. We can see the ashes and remnants of a broken life, yet God sees the beauty He can create from those ashes. We can perceive something as dead, yet God sees new life that He can bring.

What is God's perspective on what you are facing? What is Heaven's view of what's happening? Jesus wanted to transform Simon's thinking. Simon was ready to quit because, in his mind, there were no fish in his net. When Simon saw what Jesus could do, it opened his limited thinking to the realm of possibilities.

When God reveals what life can be, it changes your thinking pattern. There is a reality outside the realm of your logic and understanding. Jesus wanted Simon to experience that. Simon believed acquiring more fish would solve his problems, but Jesus understood that Simon required a complete life transformation. This starts by changing our mindset. Simon was thinking about paying bills and what would happen over the next few weeks while Jesus was planning for Simon's eternal purpose and destiny.

Simon was thinking about paying bills, while Jesus was planning for Simon's eternal purpose and destiny.

I have been a Christian for over 30 years, and the more Jesus reveals Himself to me, the more I have been repenting. I have had to repent quite a bit for my doubting and small thinking. When I solely consider my agenda, abilities, and resources, my thoughts become restricted. Instead, I must concentrate on God's limitless power, provision, and purpose. That's when everything changes.

Decisions Determine Destiny

Decisions are like dominoes when they are all standing in a row. A simple touch of the first domino affects the domino behind it until all the dominoes have fallen. It's the Domino effect. Decisions operate the same way.

As you read, you will see how Simon's future unfolded, with each decision causing a chain reaction, a domino effect. The same can happen to you. One act of obedience affects the next, and one miracle affects another.

Look at the pattern so far: Jesus instructed Simon to launch into the deep; he decided to do it. Simon experienced a miracle. This led him to repent. This elicited another invitation and instruction from Jesus.

And Jesus said to Simon, *"Do not be afraid. From now on you will catch men."* —Luke 5:10 NKJV.

In the book of Matthew, he writes about this invitation in this way.

And he saith unto them, follow me, and I will make you fishers of men. —Matthew 4:19 NKJV

What an invitation Simon was offered—an invitation to follow Jesus. Through Jesus, the life Simon was meant to live was calling him. Did Simon know what that would all entail? I propose to you that he didn't. What is a *fisher of men* anyway? There is no job description for a fisher of men on Indeed.com. There are a lot of unknowns here.

If we are going to find our future, we must realize that the invitation was, first, to follow Jesus. Our future will be revealed as we follow. We follow God step by step. We must ask ourselves, "What is my next step today?" It's easy to underestimate the power of one step because it's small. We can think steps are minimal, but it's in your step that the next aspect of your future is revealed. The right step today will lead us to where we need to be tomorrow.

The steps of a good man are ordered by the Lord: and he delighteth in his way. —Psalm 37:23 NKJV

The invitation was, first, to follow Jesus. Our future will be revealed as we follow.

God wants to order your steps. Steps imply movement. After Simon chose to follow Jesus, a domino effect was set in motion. Jesus then promised to "make" Simon and transform his life.

The word "make" doesn't mean to force someone to do something. It means to make ready, prepare, construct, form, and fashion. When we follow Jesus, we allow Him to fashion our lives for the future He has planned for us. If we are not careful, we can enable other people to fashion us for the future they think we should have.

As Jesus shapes our lives, He works to eliminate negative attitudes or behaviors that could hinder us from sabotaging our future success. I know that the devil, who is our enemy, will attack us and try to stop us from stepping into our destiny. I don't want to be the one who would sabotage my own future for lack of development.

This should be the cry of our hearts: "Lord, make and mold me into the person You desire me to be. May I decrease so You can increase in my life. Take away any attitudes and behaviors that are not pleasing to You or conducive to my future. Please help me to discern the people in my life. Show me who I need to connect with and those I need to distance myself from. Have Your way in my life, Lord!"

The word "make" also means "to be the author of a thing (to cause, to bring about)." This is so powerful because when we say "yes" to following Jesus, we essentially hand over the pen that will write the book of our lives to Jesus. Now, I am no longer the author of my own story. By following Jesus, He is the author, and my life becomes an open book for Him to write on.

As you continue reading, you will learn about Simon's remarkable and historical accomplishments because of his willingness to follow Jesus. You have probably read about Simon and the books in the Bible that he has written. I am writing about him today. Simon allowed God to author his autobiography, and Simon would make history.

Think about it: our history can be HIS STORY. Between you and God, who do you think would be able to write a more compelling autobiography? As I preach, I always encourage people to see themselves as a historical figure because you are. That it is God's intent for your life. Since He knows my future, I want my life to embody HIS STORY instead of mine.

CHAPTER 4

REDEFINING SUCCESS

It's the day every business person dreams of. Simon's business had now succeeded by surpassing all its predetermined goals. These record-breaking results exceeded all expectations. What could have been a five-year projection now happened in hours. These are the days you dream about.

What Simon chooses to do next is very significant.

"So when they had brought their boats to land, they left everything and followed him." —Luke 5:11 NLT

Wait, what did Simon do? Did Simon abandon his most prosperous and miraculous catch to follow Jesus? Yes, he did. He left all his nets, boats, and business assets. Simon had just succeeded, yet this encounter with Jesus completely reoriented his life and changed his perspective.

Define Success

Everyone must define what success means to them at some point in life. Some people aim to retire and buy a house with a white picket fence around it. For them, that's a hallmark of a successful life. But what happens after you buy the house? Is that it? Do you hang it all up and prepare for your funeral, or is there more to life than a house with a nice fence?

For others, the benchmark of success is purely financial. Once they reach a million dollars in the bank, whether they achieved it or won the lottery, they will define their life as a success. However, a National Endowment for Financial Education study found that 70% of lottery winners go bankrupt within a few years. This means that even if you achieve wealth, you can still lose it. If you define success only by your monetary gains, this will mean that you are no longer a success.

Simon and his partners have much to teach us. They gave up everything they had to follow Jesus and fulfill His purposes for their lives. Simon realized that success would be a byproduct of living for his purpose. Success should not be a goal in and of itself. It is crucial to understand this if you desire the future God has in store for you.

Simon realized that success would be a byproduct of living for his purpose.

For Simon, he realized that the supernatural results he experienced that day could only be attributed to Jesus.

This changed his values. Remember, Jesus took Simon from empty to increase and overflow. "If Jesus could do this miracle with fish, imagine what He could do with my life," Simon must have thought. It's good to remind ourselves who created all the fish in the ocean.

The Psalmist writes that our God owns it all.

> *For every beast of the forest is Mine, and the cattle on a thousand hills. I know all the birds of the mountains, And the* wild *beasts of the field are Mine.* —Psalm 50:10-11 NKJV.

Think about that. He owns the cattle on a thousand hills, an infinite supply. In Jesus, we find our infinite supply. Goals are great, but when we trust Jesus, we can go further than we even thought would be possible for us to go. God loves us when we experience this.

Simon could have expressed gratitude to Jesus and just left with his fish. But if he hadn't pursued Jesus after the miracle, he would not have become a disciple or, ultimately, the great Apostle he was destined to become. Jesus never intended His blessings and gifts to lead us away from Him. He intended His gifts to lead us back to Him, so we realize He is the source of our success and He has more for us.

"As a pastor for almost 30 years now, I have watched many people receive the answer to their prayers. Once they received what they wanted, then they quit following Jesus." Their eyes became so focused on His gifts and blessings that they never cultivated their relationship with Jesus as a disciple. A disciple is "one who engages in learning through instruction." Those who do not have a continual relationship with Jesus can miss fulfilling their purpose.

God's plan for Simon was much more vast than having a successful business day. Jesus aimed to reveal His heart to Simon, hoping that one day, Simon would carry on Jesus' ministry after His death. What a great honor. We are called to do the same.

Jesus said: *"And these signs will follow those who believe: In My name, they will cast out demons; they will speak with new tongues; they will take up serpents; and if they drink anything deadly, it will by no means hurt them; they will lay hands on the sick, and they will recover."* —Mark 16:17-18 NKJV

I am incredibly grateful for the numerous miracles Jesus has performed in my life. However, like Simon, upon reflection, I have come to understand that these miracles serve the purpose of expediting God's plans and purpose for my life rather than allowing me to become complacent and content with a life that falls short of its intended purpose.

Simon chose to prioritize following Jesus over his profits because he believed that this path would be more significant. He thought that by living a purposeful life, he could make a difference in the world and leave a lasting impact, which he considered the accurate measure of success for himself. What Jesus did for Simon that day redefined his definition of success.

Simon chose to prioritize following Jesus over his profits.

The Power Of Priorities

Our priorities are very important. Our lives today are a result of our past priorities. In truth, our priorities reveal our values.

Robert J. McKain said, "The reason most major goals are not achieved is that we spend our time doing second things first."

Did you know you can do many things in life yet still not do the one thing necessary to ensure your success? God desires to bless His children with success, but it must be done with the correct priority, as He instructed Joshua.

This Book of the Law shall not depart from your mouth, but you shall meditate in it day and night, that you may observe to do according to all that is written in it. For then you will make your way prosperous, and then you will have good success.
—Joshua 1:8, NKJV

In hard times, it's easy for our priorities to shift. But Simon's priority was the presence of Jesus and His Word, even when he had empty nets. The correct priority will give you the proper perspective. Even when it comes to challenges you are facing, you can prioritize the problem, or you can prioritize Jesus and His Presence.

The right priority will give you the right perspective.

Jesus' presence in your life will give you a different perspective on the problem. It's like flying in an airplane: the higher the altitude, the smaller everything looks. The reality is that nothing has changed in size. The houses and buildings didn't get smaller while you were flying. The freeways didn't either. What changed was your view. You are seeing everything from Heaven's perspective.

I can pursue success first, or I can prioritize seeking my God-given purpose. When I follow Jesus like Simon, I have found that my divine purpose is revealed. Then success becomes inevitable.

Having the right priorities can shape your expectations. Rather than relying on the alignment of the stars or just relationships or clients, I expect my promotion and success to come from God. The Bible assures us that promotion comes from the Lord.

For not from the east nor from the west nor from the south come promotion and lifting up. 7 But God is the Judge!

—Psalm 75:6-7, AMPC

Simon's life is a great example of this. In this book, I can only highlight some of Simon's accomplishments because he lived such an extraordinary life. Simon's priority was to live out his God-given purpose, and because of his priorities, he left behind an inspirational legacy. Have you thought about your legacy when defining success in your life? You should.

How will you be remembered? What will people say about you at your funeral? How many people's lives have you helped and touched? Simon's life is speaking to us today. Our lives will also speak beyond the grave, and what will they say?

I am very aware of this truth, which compels me to live with passion for my purpose.

Purpose Satisfies And Fulfills

Many people prioritize their personal satisfaction and fulfillment in determining how they will define success.

They ask themselves, "What satisfies me? What fulfills me?" But this mindset puts too much pressure on us to bring about own satisfaction and fulfillment. It is better to ask, "How can I please God? He made and created me; what brings joy to His heart?"

One thing I have realized throughout my life regarding personal satisfaction is that it can change. My current sources of satisfaction differ from those of years past. If we're honest, sometimes we don't know or can't fully articulate what satisfies us.

Walking in God's divine purposes brings a true sense of fulfillment and satisfaction that is long lasting. Only by pleasing God can one experience this. The difference is that now, the foundation for my fulfillment rests in God, the very source of life, love, and joy. When we put God first, He gives us the power to fulfill our purpose and live a life of significance.

Do you think Simon knew that being a Pastor or Apostle would bring such fulfillment to his life? I have never dreamed about being an author. Writing books was never a goal or on my radar until three years ago. I had no idea that writing books could bring me satisfaction, but God did. Therefore, following Jesus is crucial to living a fulfilled life because He always knows even when we don't.

Jesus, when He encountered Simon, didn't just want Simon to have an overflowing catch of fish, Jesus wanted Simon's life to overflow as well. Jesus desires for our lives to be filled with His overflowing love, joy, and peace. He wants us to experience a life that is so abundant that it spills over onto others.

Jesus didn't want Simon to just have an overflowing catch of fish, Jesus wanted Simon's life to overflow as well.

When we commit our lives to Him, He gives us the power to live a life of significance. David wrote in one of the most famous psalms, Psalms 23, about an overflowing life.

You prepare a table before me in the presence of my enemies; you anoint my head with oil; my cup overflows.
— Psalm 23:5 CSB

A cup in the Bible represents a person's life. The word "overflow" in the original language here means abundantly saturated and drenched." Notice when God brought the overflow into David's life, it was right in the middle of a battle which was a huge problem at the time. His enemies were approaching to harm him, yet instead, David's enemies had to watch God's blessing overflow in his life. When we commit our enemies to God, God has the best way to bring revenge. We don't have to do it, God does it, and He makes our enemies watch the overflow of blessings in our lives.

With God, your life can overflow, no matter what is happening around you. Therefore, it is so important that we don't gauge our lives simply by what is going on around us. For Simon, it happened right in the middle of his failure. "What Jesus did to Simon's nets and boat is what He wants to bring into your life too, so you can have a life that is overflowing." Others will see it! It will be obvious.

God will never give us a life where He is unnecessary. Unfortunately, many people make the mistake of chasing after a definition of success apart from God, living for themselves and what they can acquire. This may seem successful at first glance, but in the end, it does not bring them contentment or a sense of fulfillment.

God will never give us a life where He is unnecessary.

Jesus said, *"For what will it profit a man if he gains the whole world, and loses his own soul? Or what will a man give in exchange for his soul?"* —MARK 8:36-37

The Message Translation reads this way, what good would it do to get everything you want and lose you, the real you? What could you ever trade your soul for?

We all have heard the stories of wealthy and famous celebrities, yet they are still not fulfilled. What becomes of them? Many turn to a life of drugs and alcohol to fill their needs, which eventually ends their life prematurely. They desired fulfillment, yet their preconceived ideas of success were predicated on fame and wealth, which could not fill their void and never will.

I don't believe there's anything wrong with someone having money or recognition. But it's important to recognize that depending solely on these things for happiness will eventually lead to disappointment and depression. The scriptures tell us to seek His kingdom first, and then we will have everything we need.

But seek first the kingdom of God and His righteousness, and all these things shall be added to you.
—Matthew 6:33 NKJV

It's important to acknowledge that God desires to be the source of abundance in our lives. Only He can provide the fulfillment we crave and bring true satisfaction. If we direct our attention and efforts towards seeking God, following His teachings and intentions, the result is that He provides us with everything necessary for our life and more. Simon whose name would be later changed to Peter wrote:

As His divine power has given to us all things that pertain to life and godliness, through the knowledge of Him who called us by glory and virtue, —2 Peter 1:3NKJV

Notice that God gives us divine power that pertains to the life He has for us. There is the power to fulfill your purpose. God provides us with the strength we need to do what He is calling us to do. So many people today are exhausted and anxious because they are doing things God never asked them to do.

For me, living out my purpose results in a life of significance, not just success.

> John C. Maxwell said: *"Successful people are not always significant. But significant people are always successful."*

A Forbes article stated that many Boomers (those born between 1946 and 1964), as they begin to approach the end of their career, are looking for greater significance. Interestingly, many Millennials (between 1981 and 1996) at the other end of their careers also look for significance right out of the gate.

Success is often just associated with a title or material gains, but what truly matters is your impact on others and your contributions to their lives through Godly influence. Would you say that Simon was a success at the end of his life? He was more than just a success; he was a hero and a legend, a man who was pivotal in shaping the history of the Christian Church.

Which would you prefer to be recognized for, the amount of money you have gathered over your lifetime or the number of lives you have added value to and influenced? I understand that money is necessary for survival, but the impact you have on people's lives is what truly lasts forever. This is the true significance of success. The purpose you were created for is significant. True fulfillment happens when our God-given purpose becomes a reality.

True fulfillment happens when our God-given purpose becomes a reality.

What you were born to do is the only thing that will satisfy you. That's a success!

CHAPTER 5

THE REAL YOU REVEALED

We hear a great deal about self-esteem and self-confidence. But what is self-esteem? Self-esteem is our opinion of ourselves and our personal belief system, and at times, it can be derived from the perceptions of others or even past experiences. If a reflection of others' negative opinions drives our self-perception and our sense of identity, then our true selves will never be revealed.

We need to take a conscious look at what we are allowing to define us. When we fall into the trap of looking around instead of looking up to the one who created us, we can just become a product of our environment and culture rather than someone living out our authentic purpose.

When I was in junior high and I said something that appeared arrogant or rude, my teacher would ask this question: "Young man, who do you think you are?" What an important question. It is a question that all of us must answer. Why? The answer will define your life.

The truth is, every day, we live consistently in a way that reflects how we see ourselves. Our words, actions, and body language indicate our perceived self-worth.

This influences our relationships because people will treat you the way you treat yourself. Whether you realize it or not, you are setting the tone for how people treat you by how you view yourself.

We live consistently in a way that reflects how we see ourselves.

It's great to have friends or colleagues who think highly of you, but what you feel about yourself will always outweigh what others think. I could give you scripture after scripture about how God loves you and values you, yet in the end, what you believe about yourself will supersede what God thinks about you. The

Bible says,

"As a man thinketh in his heart, so is he." —
Proverbs 23:7 KJV.

According to Psychology Today, our identities encompass memories, experiences, relationships, and values. These components all create our identities. Studies have found that there are some common causes of identity crises.

An Identity Crisis Can Occur When:

1. **You Get Married Or Become A Parent.**
   A person will solely identify with these new-found titles.

2. **Moving From One State To Another,**
   With the changing environment, they can lose themselves in their surroundings.

3. **A Divorce Or Separation.**
   This can challenge how you define yourself, as before you were partnered with your spouse and now, they are no longer there. You ask yourself, who am I now apart from them?

4. **Loss Of A Job, Or Retirement.**
   Many people define themselves by what they do. When they are no longer employed it causes them to question their value.

5. **A Loss Of A Loved One.**
   You lose a parent, a spouse, a child. The pain of loss is tough to bear yet imagining a life without them can cause us to question our identity.

Identity Vs Roles

Understanding the difference between our identity from God and the different roles that we can take on throughout our lives is crucial to living confidently and securely while everything around us is changing.

If we depend on a position or role to secure our identity, our identity will collapse when these positions are not going well. But when we are secure in our identity in Christ, even as the roles we fulfill in this life grow unstable, we can operate without fear because our personhood is no longer attached to earthly positions.

Our real identity is always found in our relationship with God, which is secure and reliable. Our role is found in our relationship with people. Our identity in Christ can never be taken away; our roles in this world can always change. When we give our lives to Christ, He is in us, and we are in Christ, which establishes us.

Now He who establishes us with you in Christ and has anointed us is God, 22 who also has sealed us and given us the Spirit in our hearts as a guarantee.
— 2 Corinthians 1:21-22, NKJV.

The Message Translation says it this way:

God affirms us, making us a sure thing in Christ, putting his Yes within us. By His Spirit he has stamped us with his eternal pledge—a sure beginning of what he is destined to complete.
—2 Corinthians 1:21-22, MSG

The Process Of Discovery

When Jesus called his disciples, they were functioning in their individual roles and careers, yet Jesus desired for them to walk in the identity that He had for them. How does Jesus go about revealing to them who He wants them to be? He asks them a question.

Let's read how Simon discovered his identity because we can discover ours similarly.

When Jesus came into the region of Caesarea Philippi, he asked his disciples, "Who do people say that the Son of Man is?" 14 They replied, "Some say John the Baptist, others Elijah, and still others Jeremiah or one of the prophets." 15 He asked them, "But who do you say I am?" —Matthew 16:13-15 NKJV

This is the first Gallup poll ever. Was Jesus concerned with what people thought about him? No, Jesus was asking them this question because, in actuality, He wanted to reveal to them who He was. The question of who you say Jesus is, is a question everyone must answer.

The disciples responded with the thoughts and opinions of others. (Here is a classic case of the public consensus.) They said, "Well, some say," notice four different views about the same person. Some said that Jesus was John the Baptist, others said he was Elijah or Jeremiah, and others just said other prophets." I'm so thankful that Jesus didn't allow what "some say" to define Him. You shouldn't either.

If we're not careful, we can allow the "SOME SAY" crowd to hinder us from seeing who Jesus is! Some will say "Jesus heals;" others say He doesn't. Some say, "God is love." Some say, "God is mean."

The truth is Jesus was greater than what "some had said." Jesus was greater than John the Baptist, Elijah, Jeremiah, and all the prophets combined. So, what "some said" was less than who He really was. If you limit your understanding of God to what society says, you will miss the magnitude of the glorious person that Jesus really is.

The Genius Of Jesus

Simon answered, saying, "You Are The Christ, The Son Of The Living God." Simon has a revelation. God The Father revealed who Jesus is to Simon. God wants to reveal Jesus to you, too.

Simon speaks out. It took faith for Simon to say what he said yet by confessing who Jesus was activated the truth in Simon's life. Faith must have corresponding actions; confession is faith's expression.

And since we have the same spirit of faith, according to what is written, "I believed and therefore I spoke," we also believe and therefore speak, —2 Corinthians 4:13 NKJV.

This is the genius of Jesus, the reason Jesus posed the question, "Who do you say that I am?" Was to place a hunger in those listening, Simon was hungry for the answer. God met Peter at the point of his faith and desire. Is there a hunger in you to know Jesus?

We must understand that whom we say Jesus is to us is who He will be to us. The process of discovery is that, before you know who you are, you must know who Jesus is. Look at Jesus' response to Simon, and I love how the Message translation explains it,

> *Jesus came back, "God bless you, Simon, son of Jonah! You didn't get that answer out of books or from teachers. My Father in Heaven, God himself, let you in on this secret of who I really am. And now I'm going to tell you who you are, really are. You are Peter, a rock.* —Matthew 16:16 MSG

The ***process of discovery is that, before you know who you are, you must know who Jesus is.***

Jesus said when you know who I am, I will tell you who you are. It's our awareness of God that gives us the correct self-awareness. Self-awareness is a famous phrase nowadays. Do I believe it's good to examine ourselves – Yes! But I cannot find myself in myself; I must go to the one who created me.

Simon didn't find out his real identity by looking at himself. Simon discovered who he really was by having a revelation of who Jesus was first. We don't need more self-awareness; we need more revelation of who Jesus is.

If the real you is going to be revealed, we need to understand that a revelation from God reveals more than human knowledge ever will. Our human knowledge is limited. Jesus says, "Flesh and blood didn't reveal this to you, Simon." In other words, Simon, this didn't come from your human psyche or what some say; it came from heaven. The best the human mind could have figured out was that Jesus was just a prophet. Jesus told Simon, "My Father in heaven revealed it to you."

The word "reveal" in Greek means To uncover, To disclose what before was unknown. The root word means to remove a veil, manifest, or reveal a previously secret or unknown thing. As Simon is living in the deep, Jesus is uncovering the secret unrevealed purposes of God by pulling back the veil and manifesting who Simon is meant to be.

A Name Change

When Jesus first met Simon, his original name in Greek meant "reed." A reed is a plant that grows in shallow water. It is like a stick that sways when any force or wind pushes it. This plant was a pushover.

When they called Simon, they said, "Hey, reed!" Yet when Simon focused on Jesus, Jesus revealed to Simon something that was already there: he was a rock, not a reed.

This was a secret to Simon, but it was not to Jesus. On the shore that day, when Jesus saw Simon, He didn't see a reed; Jesus saw a rock. By Simon's obedience, God's secret, unrevealed purposes would be made a reality. Jesus changed Simon's name from Simon the Reed to Peter the Rock. While a reed is a pushover, a rock is solid and stable. The stone was already there, but it took Simon encountering Jesus to reveal it. The greater my revelation of Jesus, the greater my understanding of my true identity will be.

The greater my revelation of Jesus, the greater my understanding of my true identity will be.

Authority And Access

Jesus would build His church on the revelation that Peter had, the revelation that Jesus is the Christ. Peter's words have been read and spoken throughout history and will continue to be. Peter's words play an important role in church history.

Jesus continued:

> *"And I will give you the keys of the kingdom of heaven. Whatever you bind on earth will be bound in heaven, and whatever you loose on earth will be loosed in heaven."*
> — Matthew 16:19, NIV.

Our identity in Christ makes us part of His church, which the gates of hell cannot prevail against. It's so vital that you know your true identity in Christ. It can mean the difference between defeat and victory, sometimes even life and death. As children of God, He has given us keys. These keys give us access to what is available in God's kingdom. By these keys, we have the authority to walk in victory. When you know who you are, then and only then will you know what you can do.

CHAPTER 6

PURPOSES, PLANS, PASSION

The purpose is the "why" behind your existence. What you are and how you are was predetermined by God. When you don't understand your "why," what is happening around you won't make sense. God knew that the world would need what He invested in you. God could have placed you on this earth at any time in history, yet He chose this time. It's strategic.

When you don't understand your "why," what is happening around you won't make sense.

You are here to make a unique contribution to the world. Your purpose is realized when you know and understand what you were born to accomplish. It becomes the reason you get up in the morning. A person who knows their purpose will invest time, instead of wasting it. Purpose protects you from being busy yet not effective.

When our purpose is unknown, our life will be misused, so abuse is inevitable. Until purpose is discovered, our existence feels meaningless; purpose is the source of fulfillment. Abuse occurs whenever we don't use something according to its creator's intentions or design.

Where Your Purpose Began

Before you were born, your purpose originated in the mind of God. God always begins with the end in mind. This is an incredible revelation because it means that your life was never meant to be defined by who your parents were, your social status, or your circumstances. God predetermined your function and the value you would have in the world. You are priceless to God.

God spoke this to Jeremiah, whom God used as a prophet to his people:

> *Before I formed you in the womb I knew you, before you were born I set you apart; I appointed you as a prophet to the nations.*—Jeremiah 1:5, NIV.

Because we don't understand our value to God and His purpose for our life, we allow people to devalue us and put us on the discount rack. Many people live as a discounted version of themselves compared to what God wants them to be.

Jeremiah was known by God and chosen to be an instrument for Him before he came out of his mother's womb. Not only did God plan for you to be here on this earth at this exact time, but there is a specific assignment He desires you to accomplish. Notice that God sets us apart. We weren't meant to live like everyone else.

God creates us unique and original, yet because of other people's expectations or opinions, we can die a cheap copy of someone else.

For you created my inmost being; you knit me together in my mother's womb. I praise you because I am fearfully and wonderfully made; your works are wonderful, I know that full well. —Psalm 139:13-14, NIV.

The words "fearfully and wonderfully" in Hebrew mean to revere, to be held in awe, marked out, separated to be distinguished. I love that he says, "Your works are wonderful." The truth is that there was never meant to be another you, and there never will be. You were created wonderfully. When we do not fulfill our purpose, we compromise the uniqueness we were created to reveal.

Saved And Called

After living entirely for myself, feeling unfulfilled, empty, and alone, I finally committed my life to the Lord. I was 19 when I was getting ready to take my own life one evening. As a last-ditch effort, I thought I would say a prayer to God. I thought it would be like a Hail Mary pass in football to see what would happen.

I prayed, "God, if you are real, please speak to me. I will take my own life tonight if I don't hear from you. I have tried everything everyone has told me to do, and I am broken and empty."

God spoke to me that evening, saying, "You haven't tried everything. You have not tried living 100% for me." He was right. I had never even tried. I will never forget what God said next. He said, "Take your life and give it to me, and I will give you back a life you could never imagine." That night, God took the broken pieces of the life that I had left, and He did exactly what He said He would do. I am living that life now that I would have never imagined that I could live.

It's been a life beyond my wildest dreams. I could have never conjured up the idea of me being a youth minister or pastor, yet for over 20 years of my life, I have helped students heal from the pain of their parents' divorce. I have counseled many people out of suicide. I've seen thousands saved by God's power. As a youth pastor, our youth ministry would grow to over 850 students weekly. Praise God!

It was never in my projected plans to one day plant or be a founder of a new church in Murrieta California, in which I now pastor. I never saw myself writing one book, much less two books now. Our church was recently asked to broadcast our service on a national cable channel that could reach over 20 million homes.

We said yes! I know this: God is not finished with me yet, and He is not finished with you either. Never say never with God!

You are saved when you repent of your sin and invite Jesus into your heart by faith like I did that night. Heaven is now your home, and God makes you righteous. God also wants us to realize that just like He has saved us, He is also calling us. You are saved and called. God wants us to be as confident in our calling as we are in our salvation.

> *Who has saved us and called us with a holy calling, not according to our works, but according to His own purpose and grace which was given to us in Christ Jesus before time began.*
> —2 Timothy 1:9, NKJV

God wants us to be as confident in our calling as we are in our salvation.

You are not saved for the sole purpose of going to heaven. You are saved to finish your assignment on Earth. Many people think only Pastors or Missionaries are called by God. No, you are saved and called. Say it: "I am called by God!" What an honor! It's a Holy calling. The calling comes from God's purpose, given before time began. Wow! There is grace given to you by God to fulfill your purpose.

Here again, we see that there was a purpose for your life before you were born. It is the reason you were created. God calls us all, whether we are a doctor, a realtor, or working part-time at Costco. God has called you and given you a ministry. A ministry? Yes, it's to be a minister of reconciliation. Remember, Jesus told Simon, "I will make you a fisher of men."

Now all things are of God, who has reconciled us to Himself through Jesus Christ, and has given us the ministry of reconciliation, 19 that is, that God was in Christ reconciling the world to Himself, not imputing their trespasses to them, and has committed to us the word of reconciliation.
—2 Corinthians 5:18-19, NKJV.

Part of our divine purpose is to reach people for the kingdom of God. You don't have to work full-time at a church to do this. It can happen right where you are today, with the gifts and talents He has given you.

The Plan

So, what's the plan? This is one of my favorite questions to ask when we are about to plan a family outing. I would like to know the plan because it helps me to prepare. What should I pack? What time are we leaving so I can be ready?

Rest assured, God already knows the plan, even when we don't. You may be in a place where you feel lost and unsure where to go. God has a plan.

For I know the thoughts and plans that I have for you, says the Lord. They are plans for good and not for disaster, to give you a future and a hope. —Jeremiah 29:11, NIV.

God's plans always align with His purposes. If we follow His plans, which happen step by step, they will lead us to His purposes for our lives. We can have hope that His plans are good. Hope is a positive expectation of good. This reinforces our faith.

Another translation reads this way,

[11] *For I know the thoughts that I think toward you, says the Lord, thoughts of peace and not of evil, to give you a future and a hope.* — Jeremiah 29:11 NKJV

God's thoughts toward us are thoughts of peace. Having peace is vital to our well-being. The word "peace" in Hebrew means completeness, soundness, and safety; it also implies welfare, health, prosperity, and sound. Where does this peace come from? Peace emanates from God's presence. In the book of Judges, God selected a man named Gideon to rise and lead an army against their enemy, the Midianites. The Midianites were a large army. In Judges 6:24, when Gideon realized that the presence of the Lord was with him, so he built an altar there to the Lord and called it "The Lord Is Peace."

Peace is tied to the presence of the Lord. Notice it doesn't just say "The Lord who gives peace," it says, "The Lord is peace." Does He give peace? Yes, because He is peace. You have peace because the presence of the

Lord is with you. This should empower you to be bold and rest in His strength.

God revealed himself as "The Lord Is Peace" right in the middle of Gideon's problems. Gideon was faced with a terrible enemy called the Midianites. See, you can have problems and still have peace. Since peace is a person, you can have peace right in the midst of problems. Peace is not the absence of problems or trouble. Peace is not the absence of crisis; it is the presence of God right in the middle of the problem. Peace has a name, its Jesus! The apostle Paul wrote,

The peace of God, which surpasses all understanding, will guard your hearts and minds in Christ Jesus.
—Philippians 4:7, NIV

The world and our culture will try to tell you how to feel. They will say, "You should be afraid because of what's happening around you." No! The peace in you is guarding your heart and mind against what's happening around you.

The peace in you is guarding your heart and mind against what's happening around you.

God gave Gideon a strategic plan to defeat the enemy. God's presence was with Gideon, which gave him peace while he executed the plan. Gideon won the battle. We must stop being problem-focused and be presence focused. It's often our thoughts that disrupt our peace.

Isaiah wrote,

> *You will keep him in perfect peace, whose mind is stayed on you, because he trusts in you.* —Isaiah 26:3, NIV

You have peace! What happens in your thought life matters and can determine whether you experience the peace or not. When we become focused on God's presence, everything shifts. In His presence, all the odds and expectations change. All outcomes become dependent on Him and are not limited to what you can rationalize or understand.

Dealing With Detours

The detour sign is not the sign we like to see, especially when we have a critical appointment. The GPS apps on our phones often do a great job of predicting the arrival time. However, the GPS may still need to adjust, depending on when the detour happened.

Many thoughts and emotions arise from seeing that detour sign. Now, you are officially rerouted, and you may start to question the arrival time of your intended destination. Could I miss my appointment? How much time will this take?

I have realized that the road of life has detours. There can be many twists and turns along the way to fulfill our purpose. We must know that these moments can exist in life, and how to navigate them is crucial to accomplishing our goals. Even though God has a plan, unexpected circumstances may arise.

You may feel like you are in a detour right now, and the future seems uncertain. It should give us hope to know that we are not the only ones who have experienced this. It happened to Simon, the disciples, and the apostle Paul.

Detours Happen For Multitude Of Reasons:

1. God Can Bring A Detour.

When God brings about a detour, it always brings a new direction and saves you from a meaningless life.

Simon/Peter's life was rerouted from fisherman to a fisher of men because of his encounter with Jesus. God knew this detour was necessary to ensure Simon would fulfill his divine purpose.

God also detoured the great apostle Paul's life. Before he became an Apostle, he persecuted Christians and on the way to Damascus one day to kill more Christians, he encountered Jesus. Like Simon, Paul encountered God on that road and received a whole new direction and life.

2. The Devil Will Try To Detour You.

The devil's detours always lead to destruction. He is very subtle, though. He doesn't hold up a sign that says

"Detour." Instead, he places large, eye-catching billboard signs along the road of our lives that say, "Turn here." He uses temptation to lure us into sabotaging ourselves through bad decisions. He tries to deceive us into thinking that our lives don't matter and that nobody really cares about us. He is a liar.

The devil also uses sickness to try to destroy the very life that Jesus came to give us. It's important to remember that the devil is defeated because of Jesus' victory on the cross. Peter writes that healing has been made available through the stripes that Jesus bore on his back.

> *Who himself bore our sins in his own body on the tree, that we, having died to sins, might live for righteousness—by whose stripes you were healed.* —1 Peter 2:24, NKJV.

3. The Decisions Of Others Can Detour You.

In life, our choices are not the only things that affect us in life. The decisions made by others can also have an impact on our lives. You may find that you were living your life for God, yet now you are in a place you don't want to be because of something someone else did.

The Apostle Paul experienced this, and even though he had a sinful past and his life was greatly affected by the decisions of other people, he still accomplished his purpose. Paul wrote:

I have fought the good fight, I have finished the race, I have kept the faith. 8 Finally, there is laid up for me the crown of righteousness, which the Lord, the righteous Judge, will give to me on that Day, and not to me only but also to all who have loved his appearing. —2 Timothy 4:7-8, NKJV.

How Paul Dealt With His Detour

Paul was often arrested and persecuted for preaching the gospel. In one occurrence, he was arrested, and The Jews were not giving him a fair trial. Since Paul was a Roman citizen, so he pleaded to go before Caesar. His plea was granted.

In the book of Acts chapter 27, Paul was on a boat headed to Rome for his trail, but there was a considerable detour: the ship experienced an intense storm. Paul had warned them not to sail then, but they didn't listen. In the middle of the storm, Paul saw an angel.

For there stood by me this night an angel of the God to whom I belong and whom I serve, saying, 'Do not be afraid, Paul; you must be brought before Caesar; and indeed God has granted you all those who sail with you.' Therefore, take heart, men, for I believe God that it will be just as it was told to me. However, we must run aground on a certain island.'
—Acts 27:23-26, NIV

Paul, although in a storm, was pressing into the presence of God.

1. Vision Keeps The Destination In Sight.

Where there is no vision, the people perish.
—Proverbs 29:18, NIV

The angel spoke to Paul about the destination in the middle of the detour. The angel said that Paul would stand in front of Caesar. Vision is seeing with a God given revelation, not just eyesight. It is the ability to see what God sees for your life, despite the circumstance.

Remind yourself of the revelation that God has shown you. Pray for a fresh revelation of the finish line for your life today. Vision inspires and has pulling power.

2. God's Word Will Show Us The Way.

God's Word is His will. They are inseparable. Paul had the reassurance that no matter what they were seeing and experiencing in the storm, God's word would become a reality. Remember, God's word is our anchor in the deep.

Therefore take heart, men, for I believe God that it will be just as it was told to me. —Acts 27:25, NIV

We have to read and meditate on God's word daily. We need to hide His Word in our hearts when we don't need it, so it's there when we do need it. God's word brings light when the path seems dark.

Your word is a lamp to my feet and a light to my path.
—Psalm 119:105, NIV

This will help you not to forget in the dark what God told you in the light.

3. Success Happens In Steps.

We must run aground on a certain island.
—Acts 27:26, NIV

It gets worse for Paul; the ship starts to break apart. They are literally holding on to pieces of the boat. Even though the boat was fragmented, they didn't give up. They decided to move forward, even if it was just on the remains of the broken ship. They eventually washed ashore on the island of Malta.

Malta means "honey" in Greek. God created honey for man to enjoy. Honey represents abundance and provision in the Bible. Right in the middle of the detour, God can provide what you need to get you to your destination.

Although Malta was not their intended destination, it was a detour on their journey to Rome. Being on an island is better than being lost out at sea. Today, no matter what you face, you can take a step and seek God by praying, reading His Word, and doing what He asks you to do.

4. Forgiveness Is Our Defense Against Offense.

I want to remind you that Paul had done nothing wrong. He had to deal with this detour because of the decisions of others. Paul could have been bitter against them.

The people on the island received Paul well. They were very kind. They made a fire because it was cold. As Paul grabbed some sticks to put on the fire, a poisonous snake came out of nowhere and bit him. The Bible tells us that Paul was not harmed, yet he began shaking the snake off into the fire. The people on the island were watching to see how Paul would respond to all of this. Would he die from the poison?

When people wrong us and their decisions negatively affect our lives, we can quickly become offended and refuse to forgive them. Unforgiveness then turns to bitterness, which is like a poison. Someone once said, "Bitterness is like drinking poison and expecting someone else to die from it." We think that we are hurting them by not forgiving, but we are really just hurting ourselves.

> *Looking carefully lest anyone fall short of the grace of God; lest any root of bitterness springing up cause trouble, and by this many become defiled;* —Hebrews 12:15, NKJV.

Forgiveness is always a choice, not a feeling. We may not feel like forgiving, but we can choose to do it anyway. Forgiveness does not condone what the other person did to us. It simply releases them into the hands of God. The Bible tells us to forgive others as much as we have been forgiven. There are some things in life that we must shake off, just like Paul shook the snake off into the fire.

5. Serve Someone Else.

Phil, do you want me to serve someone else while I'm on a detour? This is precisely what Paul did. He had favor with one of the magistrates on the island. He learned that the man's father was very sick. Paul laid hands on him, and the man was healed. When the word got out that there was a miracle, all the sick people on the island came to Paul, and he ministered to them, and they were healed.

Paul experienced miracles in the middle of his detour because he was willing to take the focus off himself and serve others. Although Paul himself was in need, he helped take care of the needs of others. While you are waiting, wait on someone else. This is what Paul was doing by serving others. He was helping them arrive at their destination even though he had not completely arrived at his. What you do for others, God will do for you. The result?

> *They also honored us in many ways; and when we departed, they provided such things as were necessary.*
> — Acts 28:10, NKJV.

Paul arrived in Rome because of how he dealt with his detour. You will make it too! God is faithful, and even though there was a rerouting, God can bring everything back to His plans and purpose and they will prevail. God can accelerate you and make up for lost time.

Passion

Would you say you are living with passion? Passion gets you excited. You feel so strongly about something that you find yourself talking (or arguing) about it, reading about it, working on it, thinking about it, even though no one is making you.

Webster's dictionary defines passion as fervor, enthusiasm, zeal, intense emotion, and compelling action—the emotions as distinguished from a reason. Passion is love visualized and personified. Passion brings love to life.

It's when someone is passionate about what they do that it attracts attention. Passion is inspiring and contagious. We love to watch passionate people. We will pay top dollar and drive hours to see our favorite speaker, minister, sports team, and entertainer because of their passion.

Passion is created by purpose. When there is a lack of passion, we must ask ourselves if we are truly living out our life's purpose. Life was meant to be lived with passion. I have never met someone living out their God given purpose that wasn't passionate.

When there is a lack of passion, we must ask ourselves if we are truly living out our life's purpose.

The misconception about being passionate is that we think we should wait for the intense feelings to arrive, then we will live with passion. In truth, passion is a result of our choices. You chose what you are passionate about. A mentor once told me that the right decisions lead to the right emotions. You will never lack passion if you choose to live out your God-given purpose. Purpose always gives birth to hope and instills a passion for action.

Jesus' life bears this out; He was an incredible example of what it means to live passionately. During His early ministry, He would take a longer route to a city because He was passionate about reaching people.

He (Jesus) left Judea and departed again to Galilee. 4. But He needed to go through Samaria. —John 4:34 NKJV

Jesus did this for one person; she was a woman. He was drawn to minister to her. This woman was so broken, having had over five failed marriages and now on her sixth.

Interestingly, the disciples went to get food while Jesus was ministering to her. So, it was time to eat, yet Jesus was so focused on His ministry to her that food wasn't even a priority. When the disciples returned, they told Jesus He should eat; Jesus said

> *Jesus saith unto them, My meat is to do the will of him that sent me, and to accomplish his work.* —John 4:34 ASV

The Message Translation says, "Jesus said, The food that keeps me going is that I do the will of the One who sent me, finishing the work He started." Ministering to this woman fulfilled Jesus more than physical food.

Dr. Miles Monroe had so many great insights about purpose and passion. He said, "See, if you are just punching in at work and then dreaming about going to lunch, and when you get back from lunch, all you think about is punching out at five pm to go home, you haven't found your purpose yet. It's people who are not living purposefully that are the ones who can't wait to get away from what they are doing."

Dr Monroe adds, "If you can stop doing what you're doing and still be happy, you have not discovered your purpose yet. If you can just change jobs and still be happy, you haven't discovered your purpose yet." People with purpose have no working hours; they are not punching in and out. Those who live out their purpose understand it is a lifestyle not limited to working hours or even a paycheck.

Towards the end of Jesus' life, He was on trial before Pilate. This trial would determine if Jesus would live or die. Pilate asked Jesus if He was a king. Jesus responded,

> *"You say rightly that I am a king. For this cause, I was born, and for this cause, I have come into the world that I should bear witness to the truth."* — John 18:37 NKJV

Jesus said, "I was born for a cause; in other words, this cause birthed me." The cause fueled His purpose, and passion was the result. Let me ask you, what cause were you born for? Jesus knew the reason for His life, to save lost humanity, which energized His passion to the point that death would not stop it. You cannot stop a man who is not afraid of death.

The cause Jesus was born for fueled His purpose and passion was the result.

When you look up the very definition of passion in the dictionary, it clearly says the suffering of Jesus. Jesus' passion didn't fade because of the painful experience of the cross. His purpose fueled His passion so that He would die for the cause.

> *His example is this: Because his heart was focused on the joy of knowing that you would be his, he endured the agony of the cross and* conquered *its humiliation and now sits exalted at the right hand of the throne of God!* — Hebrews 12:2 TPT

Notice Jesus kept His focus on the finish line. The joy set before Him. He had passion because He was focused on the finish. The finish line was the cause and the purpose that He was born for. Jesus could have quit and given up on the cross before He finished yet keeping the vision alive in His mind through the intense suffering gave Him the passion to push past the pain. What does it take to finish? Your passion must be greater than your current pain, for this to happen you must remain focused on your purpose.

What does it take to finish? Your passion must be greater than your current pain.

Passion will always fluctuate if we try deriving our passion solely from what is happening around us instead of the purpose within us. Your purpose drives your passion, and your passion fuels your purpose. It is evident that they consistently work in partnership. Knowing what you're willing to die for, you then understand your purpose for living.

Martin Luther King Jr. said that *no one knows why they are alive until they know what they'd die for.*

Jesus and many of His followers were so passionate that they were not afraid of people's opinions, unpredictable circumstances, or even death. When purpose fuels your passion, nothing can stop you from what you were meant to do. All things begin and end with your God-given purpose. Passionate people are dangerous people because passionate people are unstoppable.

CHAPTER 7

WHAT DO YOU HAVE IN YOUR HAND?

As a pastor for over 30 years, people often ask me how to find their purpose. As we have learned, our purpose originates in God. However, many people don't understand that their purpose can be realized by asking simple questions. We see this in the life of Moses.

While living in Pharaoh's palace since birth as a Hebrew, Moses fled Egypt because he had killed an Egyptian in frustration. Moses saw how the Egyptians mistreated his people and realized that something had to be done.

Here is the first question that can help you realize your purpose:

What Frustrates You?

This injustice of the Egyptians against the Hebrews so angered Moses that it moved him. Yes, murdering an

Egyptian was wrong, but his frustration revealed the deliverer Moses was called to be.

The frustration in Moses revealed the deliverer Moses was called to be.

What frustrates or angers you can indicate your calling and purpose. If your frustration doesn't move you, than it is a simple irritation or dislike. Moses was moved by injustice. The deliverer in him was beginning to reveal itself.

What truly frustrates you? For some, seeing homeless people with no home angers them deeply. Others have seen the effects of broken homes and their impact on children, so they dedicate their lives to helping to restore them. There is a reason your heart is being moved. Don't discount it. Your calling is calling!

For me, watching people not walk in their purpose frustrates me. Seeing people waste time and experience unnecessary pain for not living out their purpose propels me to open my home to meet with people, travel and speak at events, write books, and Pastor our church. Nothing is more fulfilling to me than watching people thrive in who they were created to be. I will work endless hours to watch this happen; it's worth more than money to me!

What we can learn about our purpose is that it always involves serving other people. Your purpose is linked to a greater purpose that is bigger than you. Therefore, we must fulfill our purpose in collaboration. Nothing exists for itself; everything is related to something else.

What's In Your Hand?

Moses is now living in the wilderness, watching his father's sheep, when God appears to him in a burning bush and instructs him to return to Egypt to deliver His people. Moses was unsure that the people would believe what God had called him to do. I don't think Moses even believed he could do it, either. Look at God's response to Moses.

Then Moses answered and said, "But suppose they will not believe me or listen to my voice; suppose they say, 'The Lord has not appeared to you.'" 2 So the Lord said to him, "What is that *in your hand?" He said, "A rod." 3 And He said, "Cast it on the ground." So he cast it on the ground, and it became a serpent, and Moses fled from it. 4 Then the Lord said to Moses, "Reach out your hand and take it by the tail" (and he reached out his hand and caught it, and it became a rod in his hand), 5 "that they may believe that the Lord God of their fathers, the* God *of Abraham, the God of Isaac, and the God of Jacob, has appeared to you."* Exodus 4:1-5 —NKJV.

Here is another question we can ask ourselves that can help us understand our purpose. The question is what do you have in hand? Notice this is the question God asks Moses. There is a powerful principal here, see God uses what He has placed in our hands to lead us to what He has put in our hearts.

God uses what He has placed in our hands to lead us to what He has put in our hearts.

Moses didn't even realize that God could use what was right in his hand. He thought it was just a shepherd's rod, yet when he laid it down, it became supernatural. God put His super on Moses' natural. If we commit what is in our hands to God, God can use it powerfully. Don't despise what's in your hand.

Just like Moses, God had already invested in you the suitable DNA, giftings, and talent you need to fulfill your purpose. You are designed perfectly for your purpose. God has gifted you with what He has for you. The key is, to use what's in your hand for God's glory; don't just hold on to it; develop it and let it go.

What is in your hands to do right now? Is it a microphone, a guitar, a computer program, or a drill? What is it? What is right in front of you to do that is staring at you in the face? I'm sure there's an opportunity right now to use what's in your hand and develop it.

You may have a gift to teach, then teach if you have a voice to sing, then sing. For some of you, what is in your hand right now is a gift to do profitable business transactions for the Kingdom of God. For others, you are incredible with tools for carpentry and building. Use it for God's Kingdom. It's easy to overlook what is right in our hands. We need to value what is in our hands enough to develop it.

I have a friend named Josh, who is part of our church. He's an incredible young man. He is a project manager Monday through Friday and is successful at what he does. He has a beautiful family. He told me that God has blessed with his dream home by working in his profession (using what he has in his hand) and serving at church. He has been so amazed that he has more time to serve the church and do what God has laid on his heart for the Kingdom of God.

By Josh using what's in his hand, what God has placed in Josh's heart is being made a reality. He understands this principle. Josh is more than a project manager. He is a mighty minister and pillar in God's house. Josh is more ministry-minded now than ever and devoting more time to the Kingdom, but more importantly, he has a sense of fulfillment and passion because he knows he is fulfilling his purpose.

God always makes a deposit in you before He makes a demand. That's His grace in action. God has given you something you can use. You have been set up to succeed. "When God creates men and women, He designs them to fulfill their function and gives them specific qualities and characteristics that enable them to perform His intended purpose.

God always makes a deposit in you before He makes a demand.

These abilities were yours before birth. They do not come to you when you receive Jesus and are reborn.". God had already given Moses the tools he needed before He called him.

And the Lord said to Moses, "When you go back to Egypt, see that you do all those wonders before Pharaoh which I have put in your hand—Exodus 4 21 KJV

The Rod Of God

God used the rod that Moses had in his hand powerfully.

In Exodus 4:3: God turned his rod into a snake.

God used his rod to turn the water of the Nile to blood and to bring other plagues that would bring about the deliverance of God's people. —Exodus 7:20

God used his rod to part the Red Sea, — Exodus 14:27

As you read further in the book of Exodus, Moses' rod is now called the rod of God. When the Amalekites came to fight Israel, the rod played a significant part in the victory.

And Moses told Joshua, "Choose us some men and go out, fight with Amalek. Tomorrow, I will stand on the top of the hill with the rod of God in my hand."
— Exodus 17:9 NKJV

Moses went up on the mountain while the children of Israel fought in the valley against Amalek and the Amalekites. Moses lifted the rod. When Moses lifted the rod, they won the battle; however, God's people began to lose the battle when his arms began to tire and fall. They eventually won. I love that what started as just Moses' rod became the rod of God.

God used what Moses had in his hand to bring about a decisive victory that day. Think about it. There were hundreds of soldiers from the Amalekite army, yet God used one rod to empower His people to win, and it was in Moses' hand.

The Philistines were also the enemies of God's people, and when Samson lived, they ruled them. When one thousand Philistines attacked Samson, Samson used what was in his hand to fight. It was the jawbone of a donkey.

Then the Spirit of the Lord came mightily upon him, and the ropes that were on his arms became like flax that is burned with fire, and his bonds broke loose from his hands. 15 He found a fresh donkey jawbone, reached out his hand, took it, and killed a thousand men. 16 Then Samson said: "With the jawbone of a donkey, Heaps upon heaps, With the jawbone of a donkey I have slain a thousand men!" —Judges 15:14 -16 NKJV

Notice that the Spirit of the Lord on Samson made what he had in his hand a supernatural weapon. What an incredible miracle. One man killed one thousand soldiers with what he had in his hand.

And so it was, when he had finished speaking, that he threw the jawbone from his hand and called that place Ramath Lehi. —Judges 15:17 NKJV

Samson knew that God gave him the strength and victory. He called the place of his success Ramath Lehi, which means "the high position of illicit worship" in the Hebrew.

The story of David killing the giant Goliath is world renowned. It has been passed down from generation to generation. It's the most remarkable underdog story of all time, yet how did a boy in his younger teenage years kill a nine-foot giant named Goliath? He uses a slingshot that he has in his hand.

David went before King Saul to let him know of his desire to fight Goliath; however, King Saul tried to make David wear his armor. King Saul didn't think David could fight because of his age and size. David's response was I have not tested this armor."

So Saul clothed David with his armor and put a bronze helmet on his head; he also clothed him with a coat of mail. 39

David fastened his sword to his armor and tried to walk, for he had not tested them. And David said to Saul, "I cannot walk with these, for I have not tested them." So David took them off.
—1 Samuel 17:38,39 NKJV.

In other words, David said this armor is not what I have in my hand; it's your armor, King Saul. David did not have sophisticated weapons. He mastered what was in his hand: a slingshot.

When fighting giants, King Saul tried to clothe David in his armor. The truth is that King Saul had experience and had an opinion on how to fight. We must understand that some people will always try to clothe you in their armor. They believe that you should do it the way that they did. The armor was beautiful and strong because it was the Kings'. It looks really appealing too, yet David knew what was in his hand worked.

We cannot use what is in someone else's hand. If we do, we can devalue what God has placed in our own hands, and we will not be able to fight properly.

David knew God could use the slingshot in his hand as a mighty weapon to bring about victory because he had been using it. David told Goliath; God will deliver you into my hand.

Then David said to the Philistine, "You come to me with a sword, spear, and javelin. But I come to you in the name of the Lord of hosts, the God of the armies of Israel, whom you have defied. 46. This day, the Lord will deliver you into my

hand, and I will strike you and take your head from you.
—1 Samuel 17:45 NKJV

David told Goliath; God will deliver you into my hand.

David had a revelation of what God could do through the working of his hands. When we don't have a revelation from the Lord, the most information we can get is from other people's options. I can't fight the giant in Saul's armor. I can win if I will use what I have in my hand.

I want to live in the light of heaven's revelation, not someone's opinion of me. We must refuse to wear Saul's armor because It doesn't fit us anyway.

Every problem we face is an opportunity to use what God has put in our hands. When a problem arose for Moses, Samson, and David, the key to solving it was to use what God had placed in their hands. Remember, God uses what He has placed in our hands to lead us to what He has put in our hearts.

You Are Gifted

Every Christian is given a spiritual gift to serve and build up the body of Christ. The church is called the body of Christ.

A spiritual gift is given to each of us so that we can help each other. —1 Corinthians 12:7 NLT

God has gifted you. There is an area of your life where you are a 10. The gift God has given you is not meant just for you. It is intended to impact others. Walking in our gift may not seem like a gift because it comes so naturally to us.

When I first started public speaking, it was fun. Sure, it was a little nerve-wracking, but I gave it my all. In the early years of my ministry, a few people told me, "You have a gift for communication and public speaking." I was just having fun, honestly. It didn't seem like a big deal to me to do public speaking, but other people thought it wasn't something normal. To them, speaking in public was impossible, but for me because I had a gift It came very naturally.

Because it came more naturally to me, I was surprised when someone said it was a gift. Because I now realize what God has gifted me with, I must value and develop it. I have seen what God can do through me, with what

He gave me. In truth, it's not just a natural gift; it is God's super on my natural, however because our giftings can be like second nature to us, because it's part of our DNA, we may not recognize it, value it or develop it so we never use it.

The Apostle Paul reminded his young protégé,

Timothy, not to neglect his gift and that he should value it. One reason we can neglect our gift is because of fear. We can get intimidated because we care too much about what people think, or by looking at the gifts of others and comparing ourselves to them, we become intimidated.

Do not neglect the gift you have, which was given you by prophecy when the elders laid their hands on you.
—1 Timothy 4:14 NIV.

Paul told Timothy to meditate on it.

Practice these things, immerse yourself in them, so that all may see your progress. —1 Timothy 4:15 AMPC

"Meditate" in the original language means to care and attend to carefully. It also means to revolve in your mind and practice it. God has given us the gift, but it is our responsibility to develop the gift He has given us. We develop it by using it often to serve others.

We all must start from somewhere; what's important is that you start. Serving in a local church is a great place to use your gift. That's how I got my start.

Look at the results of developing your gifts. Paul says your progress may be evident to all. Proper practice always produces progress.

Proverbs 18:15 in the Evangelical Heritage Version says: *A person's gift opens doors for him. It leads him into the presence of great people.*

Proper practice always produces progress.

We must decide if we will rob the world or bless it with the rich, valuable, untapped resources locked away within us. Will we gift it to the world and make it a better place, or hide it and keep it to ourselves? What's in your hand? It's time to use it!

CHAPTER 8

BARRIER BREAKER

One of the biggest obstacles that limits people from accomplishing their purpose is their inability to move forward through adversity. This can begin with self-imposed limitations that derive from a limited belief system. Often, it can be our belief system that has become the barrier that is holding us back.

A limiting belief system is a mindset or conviction that you think is true and that belief limits you in some way. For example, someone who has experienced pain in a relationship may believe that all connections are painful. Although not all relationships are painful, their experience has become a mental block in their mind that limits future relational potential.

Rip The Rope

Have you ever seen a picture of a humongous elephant tied to a fence by a small rope? As you look at the picture you realize that with the mere size of the elephant, it would only take one strong kick of his foot to break the rope from the fence and allow him to run free. Why doesn't it do that? It appears to be logical and effortless for the elephant.

To understand why, you must consider what the elephant has learned over the course of his development. When the elephant was young, his owner every time the elephant moved his foot or kicked, the chain would cut his foot and cause pain. The pain became a pattern, and then one day the owner simply changed the chain for a rope as the elephant grew up. It is not the rope that ties the elephant to the fence. It is the shackle in his mind associated with past pain. The shackle in the elephant's mind is stronger than the rope around its foot. If the giant elephant kicked again now, he would rip the rope and probably shatter the fence.

The shackle in the elephant's mind is stronger than the rope around its foot.

According to the National Science Foundation, an average person has about 12,000 to 60,000 thoughts daily. Of those, 80% are harmful and 95% are the exact same repetitive thoughts.

Limiting beliefs are simply assumptions about your reality, which you draw from your life experiences. Like the elephant who thinks he can't break the rope, in actuality he can, if he can push past the pain of the past. This limiting belief would cause you to believe things like "I am not smart enough to start my own company" or "I could never write a book because no one cares about what I have to say." You lost the battle in your mind before you even started.

Then, if we do set out to try something new, we can become consumed with worry. Studies show that we often worry about things that will never happen. In a study from Cornell University, scientists found that 85% of what we worry about never happens.

85% of what we worry about never happens.

They then found that with the remaining 15%, where the event they were worried about, did happen, 79% of the subjects discovered that either they were able to handle the difficulty better than expected or the problem taught them a lesson worth learning. The conclusion is that 97% of our worries are baseless and result from an unfounded pessimistic perception.

Self-imposed limitations are limiting our beliefs, and they are nothing more than rules that we have created in our heads. Rules that need to be broken!

Cross The Threshold

You were created to be a barrier breaker. It's time to cross the threshold. A threshold is a limit at which an arrangement changes. It is the point of departure or transition. It is the level at which you start to experience something, or something starts to happen.

This is what I love about Peter. He is willing to launch out into the deep. He will take risks. He will try something new. Peter will break a barrier that no other human will.

It is essential to understand that storms will arise whenever you launch into deep waters. When you set out to fulfill your purpose, there will be opposition. As Peter and the disciples followed Jesus and did what Jesus had called them to do, they found themselves in the middle of a storm.

> *Immediately Jesus made His disciples get into the boat and go before Him to the other side, while He sent the multitudes away. 23. And when He had sent the multitudes away, He went up on the mountain by Himself to pray. Now when evening came, He was alone there. 24. But the boat was now in the middle of the sea, tossed by the waves, for the wind was contrary. 25. Now in the fourth watch of the night Jesus went to them, walking on the sea. 26. And when the disciples saw Him walking on the sea, they were troubled, saying, "It is a ghost!" And they cried out for fear.* —Matthew 14:22-26 NKJV

Matthew writes in his gospel that they were in the middle of the sea, inside the storm. Their position is significant for a couple of reasons. Think about it: a storm arises right in the middle of doing what God calls them to do. As you read further about acceleration, I will show you another reason why this is significant.

This storm was intense. It was dark and probably around 4:00am in the early morning. The storm was violent enough that they were being tossed back and forth. The barriers in life always want to capitalize on and reinforce your limitations. This is no time to be passive. With Jesus, we can progress, move beyond the boundaries, and break the barriers.

There are three barriers we must break to cross the threshold in our lives, yet you will also experience three incredible benefits once you have broken through. We see this in Peter's response to the storm.

The 1st Barrier Is: The Fear of the Unknown.

What barrier are you facing? As a teenager, I was overwhelmed with anxiety which caused me to have migraine headaches that resulted in my mouth going numb. I ended up in the emergency room many times. I had no idea what would become of my life and our family. I thank God that He has healed my heart and restored my mind. Our family eventually healed from the effects of the divorce.

A storm can be overwhelming. The disciples were afraid. They thought they saw what looked like a ghost in the distance, on the surface of the water. But it wasn't a ghost. It was Jesus! He was coming to help them. Fear can take something meant to be good and turn it into something terrible. Notice that Jesus comes to them in the storm and addresses their fear. He says, "Do not be afraid!" One translation says to take courage.

But immediately, Jesus spoke to them, saying, "Be of good cheer!
— Matthew 14:27 NKJV.

Fear can take something meant to be good and turn it into something terrible.

I love this. Jesus says, "Be of good cheer!" So many people have a fixed idea of what Jesus is like. They put God in a box. But in reality, Jesus came to them in a form they had never seen before. He was walking on the water. This is something that the disciples had never seen before. Do you believe that Jesus can do something in your life that you have never seen done before? I do!

I believe Jesus shows us by walking on the water that just because something has never been done before doesn't mean it can't be done. You just haven't seen it yet.

Don't let fear talk you out of breaking the barrier! Fear will make the barriers seem bigger than they are. We must stop magnifying the size of the barriers and start looking at the size of our God. God is greater than any barrier we face.

> *For God has not given us a spirit of fear, but of power and of love and of a sound mind.* — 2 Timothy 1:7 NKJV.

Fear will rob you of power and the ability to love. Fear always makes your mind unstable. Did you know the Bible has 365 "fear not" scriptures? That's one for each day of the year. It is strategic that God put many scriptures in the Bible on fear because it means fear will try to come to you daily. Say to yourself, "No fear here!"

The 1st Benefit Is: A New Vision.

Jesus walking on the water must have been a sight to see! God loves to give us glimpses of what life can be with Him. Jesus wanted them to see the realm of possibility! Our God can defy nature. Jesus shows us that we don't need what we thought we needed to overcome the storm; what we need is Him.

You need a new vision. A vision of you doing what you thought you couldn't do. A picture of you breaking the barrier you thought was impossible. Can you see yourself breaking through? What does a victorious you look like? What do you look like when you are fully walking in faith? If you can't see it, you'll never achieve it. Peter is so inspired that he asks to join Jesus on the water.

"Lord, if it is You, tell me to come to You on the water."
—Matthew 14:28 NKJV

Second Barrier Is:
Getting Out Of Your Comfort Zone.

If Peter were to walk on water, he would have to go against everything he had ever learned about boats and about the ocean, and he would have to place his trust in Jesus. The boat represents the comfort zone. "I'm in deep waters and the storm, but I'm in the boat, so I'm safe. My confidence is in the boat."

In the storm, Peter believed he would be more secure walking on the water with Jesus than in the boat. For this to happen, Peter had to change his perspective about the storm in order to be able to walk over it. Change is essential for growth. You can't break barriers if you believe the storm is greater than the God you serve.

In the storm, Peter believed he would be more secure walking on the water with Jesus than in the boat.

You must step outside of your comfort zone. Comfort is like a drug. It's addictive. Our comfort zone is where our dreams go to die. Growth can only happen outside the comfort zone. If you're not feeling uncomfortable regularly, it's a good indication that you're not growing.

Stepping into a new season, a new job, or a new relationship isn't easy. It's awkward because you've never experienced it before. I like to say, "Lean into the awkward. Don't walk away from it." That's where you grow.

We love our comfort zone because it's where we are in total control. God can't be in control of your life if you try to be in full control of it. Your comfort zone will keep you stagnant. We must fight against living a stagnant life. It can become habitual. You may not even realize it, but if you accept it long enough, it will become your life. Then you lose hope, give up on dreams, and quit on your future.

God didn't save you so you could be safe. He saved you so you would be dangerous. Believe it!

2nd Benefit Is: Barriers Break.

Jesus says, "Come!" What an invitation! Jesus knew Peter could do it, or He would not have invited him. Peter got out of the boat and walked on the water! A barrier in his life was broken. Peter experienced something new! It didn't matter what others would say or think at this point. He was doing it!

Peter took a risk and walked above the storm. In truth, Peter walked on the word he heard from Jesus. One word, "come," was enough for Peter to act and walk on water. When we walk on Jesus' words, we too will walk above the storm. When the words from Jesus came to Peter, faith came to Peter. Faith is not just believing; it is acting on what you believe. James writes that faith without works is dead.

"Thus also faith by itself, if it does not have works, is dead. 18 But someone will say, 'You have faith, and I have works.' Show me your faith without your works, and I will show you my faith by my works." — James 2:17-18 NKJV

James emphasizes that you can see faith by its corresponding actions. Some say you have faith, but it hasn't changed your actions. In that case, it is just a belief. You can believe that you can break every barrier that is in front of you, but until you take a step and make a move toward the barrier to break it, it will never break.

If you say you have faith, but it hasn't changed your actions, it's not faith.

Peter experienced the miraculous. We are to walk in the words of Jesus as well. His words have the power for you to walk above any storm. You are meant to be a water walker.

I don't know what barriers have been interfering with your life, whether they have been self-imposed or placed on you by others. With Jesus, you can break through any barrier.

But when he saw that the wind was boisterous, he was afraid; and beginning to sink, he cried out, saying, "Lord, save me!"
—Matthew 14:29-30 NKJV

3rd Barrier Is: "Fear Of Failure!"

When Peter first stepped onto the water, it's important to note that the storm was already raging. There was a lot of wind and waves, yet he was already walking on the water. So, what changed then that caused Peter to begin to sink, if the wind and the waves didn't change? Peter's focus changed when he took his eyes off Jesus, the author and finisher of our faith. Remember, Jesus makes our faith perfect!

Peter doubted when he got distracted. We can see here just how dangerous being distracted can be. See, faith has a focus. Peter's focus started to change, so his belief system changed. Logic began to set in, causing him to think, "Wait, I can't walk on water. That's impossible," even though he was already in the process of doing it.

Peter doubted when he got distracted.

Therefore, the Bible commands us to walk by faith, not by sight. It should be a lifestyle of faith because more barriers may arise. If you can break one barrier, you can break them all. What you see can change, but faith lives by what it believes despite what it sees. It doesn't matter what the wind and waves are doing. Our focus should be on Jesus.

"For we walk by faith, not by sight."
— 2 Corinthians 5:7 NKJV

The apostle Paul wrote that faith isn't just a good concept; faith is a law. Just as we can expect the law of gravity to work constantly, so will the law of faith.

"Where is boasting then? It is excluded. By what law? Of works? Nay, but by the law of faith."

— Romans 3:27 NKJV

Some people think, "Why try anything new? Why risk it? I might fail." I'm here to tell you, yes, you probably will make some mistakes along the way. However, you'll never know what you can do until you try and take the risk.

When my wife and I prayed about moving from Texas to California to plant a new church, we thought, "What if we move to another state and fail?" But there was another thought and it was, "What if I never try? If I never try, I will never know my potential." I don't know if I could live with myself, if I was always wondering what my life could have been like if I had not gone.

I would rather have tried and failed than never have tried at all. Thank God, He has been so faithful to us! Our church is growing, and we are breaking barriers. We have been living this miraculous life of faith and have been walking on water for over 11 years now with our church. God is faithful!

Some may want to focus only on Peter's failure, but Peter was the only man besides Jesus to have ever walked on water...in the history of the world. The disciples in the boat may have laughed and ridiculed him, but like Peter, I would rather be a wet water walker than a dry boat talker any day!

As Peter is sinking, he cries out to Jesus,

> *"And immediately Jesus stretched out His hand and caught him, and said to him, 'O you of little faith, why did you doubt?"*
> — Matthew 14:31 NKJV

Notice Jesus stretched out his hand immediately and caught him; this means Peter was so close to Jesus, only an arm's length away. Jesus rescues Peter and then gives him instructions. Jesus says, "Oh ye of little faith, why did you doubt?" When you understand how the original Greek language translates this, the focus is not on the size of Peter's faith but the endurance of it. In other words, the same faith Peter had to start was enough for him to finish.

3rd "Benefit" Is: You Experience Growth.

Peter grew in so many ways that day. It is God's will for you to grow. However, just because it is God's will for you to grow doesn't mean you will. Growth must be intentional. Jesus instructed Peter to come, but it was up to Peter to take the step. Only Peter responded out of the eleven other disciples. You may be the only one in your family or group of friends that chooses to grow; do it anyway. At times, we need to be willing to go alone. Yet we are not alone because Jesus is walking with us!

Are you growing? We must commit to growth. Growth is only possible with commitment. The areas in which you are growing are the areas you have committed to.

Let me ask you: Where will you be one year from today? Will the same problems plague you, or will you move forward and break barriers? Don't leave growth up to chance; choose to do it! What incredible blessings and new opportunities await you on the other side of the barriers? It's time to break them in Jesus' name!

Don't leave growth up to chance; choose to do it!

Sudden Acceleration

Another way God can break barriers in our lives is by accelerating time. This is your year for acceleration! Regarding God's purposes for our lives, God can accelerate time to make His plans a reality. God can make up for losses extraordinarily! The swift arrival of new relationships and opportunities can be orchestrated by God miraculously, much like how Jesus intervened and transformed Peter's business from having empty nets to overflowing ones in a matter of hours. That's acceleration!

God is always on time. Sometimes, I would like Him to be a little early, but He is never late. He may seem to work slowly, but a slow period can turn suddenly. The word suddenly is mentioned in the Bible 71 times; it's cited 44 times in the Old Testament and mentioned 17 times in the New Testament. The word suddenly comes from the Greek word 'aphno,' which means unaware or unexpected. There is an unexpected turnaround coming your way!

We read about Peter walking on the water in the writing of Matthew, but Mark and John's accounts do not mention Peter walking on the water. I think it was because they were jealous; they didn't get out of the boat. I'm kidding.

Mark and John add more perspective to what happened in that storm in their books of the Bible. Mark writes that Jesus saw them rowing. They were doing what they knew to do, but it wasn't getting them the desired result.

Mark writes that Jesus would have passed them by. It means that Jesus planned to go to the other side, which was the intended goal, yet He saw the disciples straining in their strength and heard their cries. Jesus doesn't just leave them there – He goes to them.

Never hesitate to cry out to God, no matter what the situation is. Our God allows us to interrupt Him. We can get into this thought process that God's purposes are so vast that He doesn't care that we are striving in a storm and not getting anywhere.

He does see us striving! It's not enough to just strive; the disciples realized they must cry out. John writes in more detail about the time in the storm.

So when they had rowed about three or four miles, they saw Jesus walking on the sea and drawing near the boat; and they were afraid. —John 6:19 NKJV

Remember, Matthew wrote they were in the middle of the sea because of the storm. The Sea of Galilee is pear shaped and is about 7 miles wide. They should have been further along, but because of the storm, they were stuck.

Did you ever feel like you should be further along in life because of circumstances that have arisen? Do you feel like you have been striving yet still stuck?

John writes something that Mark and Matthew didn't mention.

Then they willingly received Him into the boat, and immediately the boat was at the land where they were going.

—John 6:21 NKJV

Look what the disciples did; they willingly received Jesus into the boat. We must receive Him willingly into the boat of our lives, or else we will keep straining and stay stuck.

The boat immediately got to the other side when they willingly received Him. They went from the middle of the sea to the shore immediately. That's an unusual acceleration that only Jesus can bring into our lives.

They went from the middle of the sea to the shore immediately

---

What the disciples couldn't do in their strength, Jesus did immediately! The barrier that they couldn't break themselves, Jesus broke for them. Jesus accelerated them to where they needed to be at the right time despite the storm, setbacks, and barriers. Acceleration is coming to your life! With Jesus, you are a barrier breaker!

CHAPTER 9

A DEEPER LOVE

How vital is love to our lives? It is essential for our well-being because we were created to be loved and love others. We were created for God, and God is love. 1 John 4:16 says, *"God is love."*

God doesn't just commit acts of love; His character is love. God's love is not based on what we do or don't do. Love is who He is. This is fascinating to me because God loves you because He chooses to. God doesn't need us; He wants us. He wants us to live loved. Studies have found that the feelings associated with love and affection appear to carry numerous health benefits, such as lowering your blood pressure, stabilizing your mood, and much more.

God told Adam that after He created him, it was not good for man to be alone, so He created Eve. We weren't meant to live in isolation. We were designed not only to receive love but to give love.

Jesus said, *"'Love the Lord your God with all your heart and with all your soul and with all your mind.' This is the first and greatest commandment. And the second is like it: 'Love your neighbor as yourself.'"* —Matthew 22:37-39 NKJV

According to Jesus, you cannot love anyone beyond your love for yourself. You can only love someone else to the same degree that you love yourself. Therefore, it is more crucial for you to love yourself than to love me. When you love yourself, I am safe. Whatever you hate about yourself, you will hate about everybody else, because you cannot love beyond your love for yourself.

According to Jesus, you cannot love anyone beyond your love for yourself.

Loving Yourself

How do we love ourselves? We love ourselves by understanding that love does not start with us; it begins with God loving us first. We must first receive God's love for us in the deepest depths of our hearts, then God's love will flow through us.

John was the disciple who had a revelation of Jesus' love. John wrote about himself that he was the disciple whom Jesus loved. Not because Jesus loved John more than the others but because John loved Jesus more. See, John loved Jesus so much because John knew and understood Jesus' love for him. This is vital to understand our relationship with God.

When John wrote in the scriptures, he used the word beloved. In other words, he always encouraged people to be loved by God. Allowing God to love us first is the first step to loving ourselves. John writes,

> *Herein was the love of God manifested in us, that God hath sent his only begotten Son into the world that we might live through him.* — 1 John 4:9-11 ASV

Look at how the Easy-to-Read Bible Translation writes it,

> *True love is God's love for us, **not our love for God**. He sent his Son as the way to take away our sins.*
> —1 John 4:10 ER

Was John saying that our love for God is not essential? No, our love for God is important because we are commanded to love God, yet our love for God isn't first; love originated in God first. Once we receive God's love, we can not only love ourselves, but we can also love God. We love God back with the love He first gave us. This is brilliant. God set it up this way. We can even love our enemies with God's love flowing through us.

We love God back with the love He first gave us.

Jesus Speaks Of His Death

I can't imagine what this conversation was like to hear. Jesus began talking about His death to his disciples. Peter and the disciples had left everything to follow Jesus. It had been three years of living, laughing, and crying together. They had seen so many miracles, including people raised from the dead. Now their friend and hero was talking about His death. Jesus warns them about what will come and how their lives will be affected.

Then Jesus told them, "All of you will be made to stumble because of Me this night, for it is written: 'I will strike the Shepherd, and the sheep of the flock will be scattered.' 32. But after I have been raised, I will go before you to Galilee." 33. Peter answered and said to Him, Even if all are made to stumble because of You, I will never be made to stumble." 34. Jesus said to him, "Assuredly, I say to you that this night, before the rooster crows, you will deny Me three times." 35. Peter said to Him, "Even if I have to die with You, I will not deny You!"– Matthew 26:31-35 NKJV

I love Peter. He is such a passionate guy. (You can be passionate and still be wrong.) When He hears the news of Jesus dying. Peter starts to boast about what he's going to do. Literally, with other disciples right there, it's like he's pointing to them, saying, "Even if this causes everyone else to stumble (Meaning you guys). I will never be made to stumble."

Peter says, "Even if I have to die with you, Jesus, I will never deny you." Jesus responds, "Tonight, you will deny me not three times." Ouch! Later that very evening, it happened exactly as Jesus said it would.

Once they came to the garden of Gethsemane and arrested Jesus, Peter followed them and went to the palace. While there, a little girl asked Peter if he was with Jesus, and Peter said "No!" and denied Him. Then a woman asked him, and again he said, "No!" Finally, some people asked Peter if he had been with Jesus, and he said no, and the roaster crowed three times.

Mistaken Beliefs About Love

When the pressure of persecution was applied, Peter gave into fear. He succumbed to the temptation to deny his relationship with Jesus. We must understand how fear and love intertwine. Peter had misguided beliefs about love that caused him to yield to temptation instead of overcoming it.

Let's Study These Beliefs And Learn.

1. Peter Believed That God's Love Was Earned.

By Peter boasting about his love for Jesus and stating that he would die for Him, Peter somehow thought he would earn Jesus' love.

2. Peter Was Relying On His Own Love For God.

This is a critical mistake that Peter and many people make. Peter depended on his love for Jesus instead of Jesus' love for him. The problem is that our love for God fails in times of pressure and temptation, but God's love for us never fails.

Our love for God fails in times of pressure and temptation, but God's love for us never fails.

Peter denied Jesus because Peter was relying on himself. We can succumb to temptation when solely relying on our love for God. Peter's love for God failed, but this is key: God's love for Peter didn't fail! If we're going to have a deeper love, we must understand that my love for God flows out of His love for me. Many people, just like me, have heard and read this scripture:

> *And you must love the Lord your God with all your heart, all your soul, and all your strength.*
> —Deuteronomy 6:5 NKJV

As a young Christian, I wanted to live out this scripture. I wanted to love God with everything I had, so I would try hard to do it. The problem was that I still loved other things way more than I loved Jesus. I wondered if this scripture was even possible. I was frustrated and then I just wanted to give up.

We must understand that we cannot give what we have not received. Before you can love God with all your heart, you must first receive His love in your heart. The focus should be on receiving before giving.

Growing up, when I heard Deuteronomy 6:5 preached in church, the emphasis was always on "YOU." The focus should never be on me first because I fail. When we teach about God's love, the focus should be on God's love for us rather than our love for Him. Remember, your love for God, flows out of His love for you.

A Perfect Love

Peter was fearful when persecution presented itself. Fear can be the result of the unloved areas of our lives. John writes,

> *There is no fear in love, but perfect love casts out fear because fear involves torment. But he who fears has not been made perfect in love.* —1 John 4:18 NKJV

The word "perfect" means: To carry through ultimately, to accomplish, finish, and to bring to an end. Fear has torment: It means punishment and penalty. So, could it mean that people who won't allow God to love them fully, have areas of their lives that they feel "unworthy," so they secretly punish themselves?

God so loved you that He sent His son to be punished and die for your sins. What's so beautiful is that since

Jesus was punished, you won't have to punish yourself anymore. Fear and love cannot coexist! Peter and John both had different beliefs when it came to God's love.

When You Compare Peter and John:

1. Peter Boasted About His Love For God.
John wrote about Jesus' love for him.

2. Peter Tried To Earn Jesus' Love.
John would lay His head on Jesus' chest and receive His love.

3. Peter Denied Jesus And Couldn't Be Found While Jesus Was Suffering On The Cross.

John was the only disciple out of the twelve to be at the foot of the cross. John didn't buckle under the pressure of persecution. John wrote the powerful scripture that there is no fear in love. John lived like he was loved because he knew how much Jesus loved him.

Look at the areas in your life that you still have fear in, and it's in these areas that you have not fully received the love of God. We must let God's perfect love cast out fear. There is no fear in love.

What's interesting about John is that they couldn't kill him. Historians write that he was exiled to the island of

Patmos to die, because they tried boiling in hot oil, and he would not die.

Faith Works By Love

When God calls us into the deep, it requires faith. Faith to believe that what Jesus has said will come to pass. Faith is easy when you know you're loved.

But faith working through love.
— Galatians 5:6 NKJV

The word "works" means to be operative, be at work, and put forth power. Many people struggle in their faith walk because they struggle to receive God's love. Faith comes by hearing God's word, yet it works and operates by love.

Although Peter denied Jesus, Peter did repent. When Jesus rose from the dead, He wanted to ensure Peter knew about the Resurrection. He wanted Peter to know that he was still loved even when Peter's love failed. The angel said to make sure that Peter knew Jesus was alive.

But he said to them, "Do not be alarmed. You seek Jesus of Nazareth, who was crucified. He rises! He is not here. See the place where they laid Him. 7 But go, tell His disciples—<u>and Peter</u>—that He is going before you into Galilee; there you will see Him, as He said to you." —Mark 16:6-7 NKJV.

There is a deep and perfect love available for you and me. We can only find it in our Lord and Savior Jesus.

God truly loves you! There is no other deeper love that you can experience than the love of God. When you receive it, you can stand against any temptation or persecution. Allow yourself to BE LOVED.

CHAPTER 10

THE POWER TO BE

Our society values achievements and places great importance on accomplishments. Living in today's world means being bombarded with messages that promote the idea that what you do determines your value. There is a strong emphasis on doing.

We greet people by asking, "How are you doing?" If the conversation continues, we may ask them what they do for a living. Based on their employment, we can try to assess their value. We can constantly reinforce the idea that what we do creates our being. However, we are not human doings; we are human beings.

The priority is now that, what I do comes first, and then it will determine what I will be. Religion reinforces this. Religion teaches that our behavior (our doing) can earn us (our being) right standing with God. The problem is that we could never do enough to earn our right standing with God. We cannot make ourselves holy or righteous. This is impossible!

With this mindset, so many people feel like hamsters on a hamster wheel, doing a lot and giving a ton of effort, yet never really having true fulfillment or advancement. There is a better way!

The spiritual life, which is your internal world, is a life that depends on Christ to do in us that which we cannot do for ourselves. God's priority is to transform your inner being, which will change what you do. Therefore, your "doing" is a product of your "being." I like to say it this way: Your internal world, what is happening inside you, now dictates what happens in your behavior (the outer world).

The apostle Paul wrote:

> *Therefore, if any man be in Christ, he is a new creature: old things are passed away; behold, all things are become new.*
> —2 Corinthians 5:17 KJV

When we invite Jesus Christ into our hearts by faith and repent of our sins, we are in Christ, and Christ is in us! The word "creature" in Greek means "a new creation," a new being. This is powerful! God makes all things new in our lives. When our internal being is transformed it works out of our lives, the doing, for God.

The Promise For Purpose

After Jesus' death and resurrection, He spent 40 days showing the world He was alive. He walked the streets and ministered to His disciples. Before Jesus ascended to heaven, He assured His followers that they would not be alone and that He would send His Holy Spirit to comfort them.

While Jesus was on earth, He could only be in one place at a time because He was clothed in human flesh. If you were not near Jesus or in the area where He was, or if someone connected to you did not come on your behalf to see Jesus, you would not have seen Him or experienced his ministry.

When Jesus ascended to heaven, the Holy Spirit would be sent to be with us, and He would be in all places at once. Jesus said,

Nevertheless, I tell you the truth; it is expedient for you that I go away: for if I go not away, the Comforter will not come unto you; but if I depart, I will send him unto you.
—John 16:7 KJV

You and I are not alone; we have the Holy Spirit as our comforter and helper. A comforter in the original language is "Paraklētos," which means: summoned, called to one's side, especially to one's aid. One who pleads another's cause with one, an intercessor. He is your comforter!

Jesus would charge them to continue the ministry He started. Jesus said to them previously,

Very truly I tell you, whoever believes in me will do the works I have been doing, and they will do even greater things than these, because I am going to the Father. —John 14:12-14 NIV

Jesus not only gave instructions to His followers on what they would do, but Jesus spoke precisely how they would go about doing it.

And being assembled together with them, he commanded them not to depart from Jerusalem, but to wait for the promise of the Father, "which," he said, "you have heard from me; 5.for John truly baptized with water, but you shall be baptized with the Holy Spirit not many days from now." 6.Therefore, when they had come together, they asked him, saying, "Lord, will you at this time restore the kingdom to Israel?" 7. And he said to them, "It is not for you to know times or seasons which the Father has put in his own authority. 8 But you shall receive power when the Holy Spirit has come upon you; and you shall be witnesses to me in Jerusalem, and in all Judea and Samaria, and to the end of the earth." —Acts 1:4-8 NIV

Notice that the purpose that God had for Peter and the disciples to be fishers of men would mean that they would continue the ministry of Jesus by the power of his Holy Spirit. We are called to do the same. Wherever role you find yourself in today, whether a stay-at-home mom or dad, accountant, teacher, school principal, or construction worker, we are called to be ministers of reconciliation and continue the ministry of Jesus.

Jesus doesn't overlook our doing; He does speak of doing His work. It is called the work of the ministry, yet He doesn't command His disciples to do what He did without the empowerment of the Holy Spirit.

Jesus doesn't command His disciples to do what He did without the empowerment of the Holy Spirit.

The promise of the Father was the gift of the Holy Spirit. Notice Jesus instructs them not to leave Jerusalem until they receive the promise, which would give them the power to fulfill their purpose.

In other words, don't try to DO it without BEING empowered first. The disciples did as Jesus instructed.

The Bible says:

And when the day of Pentecost had fully come, they were all with one accord in one place. And suddenly there came a sound from heaven as of a rushing mighty wind, and it filled the whole house where they were sitting. And there appeared to them divided tongues, as of fire, and one sat upon each of them. And they were all filled with the Holy Spirit and began to speak in other tongues, as the Spirit gave them utterance.
— Acts 2:1-4 NIV.

The scripture says they were all filled! Being filled with the Holy Spirit empowers us to be the witnesses Jesus told us to be. It's important that Jesus wasn't asking them to witness; he said, "BE A WITNESS." When this happens, your lifestyle as a witness indicates that you belong to him.

My friends, if Peter and the other disciples, after spending three years with Jesus and experiencing all of the incredible miracles, needed the baptism of the Holy Spirit, so do we.

The Holy Spirit's Work

So you may ask, Phil, "I have asked Jesus into my heart. Don't I already have the Holy Spirit?" Yes, you do. You cannot be saved unless the Father draws you by His Holy Spirit.

No one can come to me unless the Father who sent me draws him. And I will raise him up on the last day.
—John 6:44 ESV

The Work of the Holy Spirit:

When We Are Saved:

1. **The Holy Spirit Works An Inner Work First.**

Jesus said,

The Spirit of truth, whom the world cannot receive because it neither sees him nor knows him. But you know him, for he dwells with you and will be in you.
— John 14:17 NKJV

When the Holy Spirit Baptizes Us:

2. **The Holy Spirit Does An Outer Work.**

Let me give you this illustration: If I have a nice cold bottle of water in my hand and drank it, it will quench my thirst, filling my stomach. However, there is a difference between drinking from a water bottle and going and jumping in the ocean.

Drinking a bottle of water is what the Holy Spirit does when we get saved. It is an inner work; however, when He baptizes us, it is like jumping into the ocean and submerging in it. This is the outer work. The inner work of the Holy Spirit will save you for heaven, but the baptism of the Holy Spirit will give you the power to live on earth to help you see others saved.

Bill Johnson said, "The Holy Spirit comes in you for you, but He comes on you for others."

The Power For Purpose

Jesus said we would receive power when the Holy Spirit comes upon us. The word "dynamis" in Greek means strength, power, ability, or capability. The Holy Spirit will give you strength and ability and make you capable of living out the purpose God has provided you.

There are two kinds of power that the Holy Spirit gives us:

1. **Moral Excellence.**

The word "dynamis" also means moral power. This means that the Holy Spirit empowers us to live a holy life. We can be like Christ in our actions because the

Holy Spirit empowers us. Notice that acting Holy (Or Doing) comes from being Holy.

2. The Power To Perform Miracles.

The word "dynamis" also means the Power to perform miracles. Peter's life was impacted once again when the Holy Spirit was poured out on him and the other disciples. When they came out of the upper room, some people mocked them.

Peter addressed them and began to preach his first sermon. He spoke with conviction and boldness, and three thousand people were added to the church that day. What a miracle! Peter's life became a witness to the power of the Holy Spirit.

As he addressed the crowd, Peter would speak to future generations like us to ensure that we knew the promise of the Holy Spirit is still for us today. Peter said,

> *"For the promise is to you and to your children, and to all who are afar off, as many as the Lord our God will call."*
> —Acts 2:39 NKJV

Just like salvation, the promise of the Holy Spirit's baptism must be received by faith. There is a prayer in the last chapter of this book that you can pray to receive Jesus and receive this promise of the baptism of the Holy Spirit.

Deeper Prayer

Not only was power and boldness a result of the baptism in the Holy Spirit, but so was the way they spoke. The Scripture tells us they spoke in other tongues. It was a heavenly language.

And they were all filled with the Holy Spirit and began to speak in other tongues, as the Spirit gave them utterance.
—Acts 2:4 NKJV

Notice that all who were there were filled and spoke in other tongues. In Acts 19:2, the Apostle Paul asked some people if they had received the Holy Spirit when they believed. They had not.

And when Paul had laid his hands upon them, the Holy Spirit came upon them; and they spake with tongues and prophesied.—Acts 19:6 KJV

Again, when the Holy Spirit came upon them, they began to speak in tongues. These tongues spoke on the day of Pentecost when they were baptized in different dialects so people could witness the power of God in their native language. This happened publicly. Speaking in tongues is a gift that also enables us to pray supernaturally. Not only can it be voiced publicly, as it was then. It is to be used as we pray as well. This will take your prayer life deeper.

Let me give you four reasons why speaking in tongues in prayer, is important.

1. It Is A Sign That We Believe.

Jesus said,

> *And these signs will follow those who believe: In My name, they will cast out demons; they will speak with new tongues;*
> —Mark 16:17 KJV

The word "sign" means a mark or token—by which a person or a thing is distinguished from others and is known. Notice Jesus said that we would speak in new tongues.

2. Our Spirit Prays.

When we pray in tongues, The Holy Spirit prays through our spirit the perfect prayer that needs to be prayed at that time. Our prayer begins to come from a much deeper place than our intellect. In the scriptures, praying in tongues is called praying in the spirit.

> *For if I pray in an unknown tongue, my spirit prayeth, but my understanding is unfruitful.* —1 Corinthians 14:14 KJV

There are times in life when we will have prayed everything we know how to pray with our mind; the great news is that we are not just limited to our minds. Our spirit can pray. This benefits us because the Holy Spirit comes alongside us to pray the perfect prayer that we don't know to pray.

Paul also tells us that when we pray in tongues, we pray directly to God, not to men.

For anyone who speaks in a tongue does not speak to men but to God. —1 Corinthians 14:2 NKJV

This means the devil himself cannot understand us when we pray in the Spirit.

It Builds You Up.

He that speaketh in an unknown tongue edifieth himself, but he that prophesieth edifieth the church.
—1 Corinthians 14:4 KJ21

Edify means to build up. There will be days when you won't have anybody around you to encourage you or build you up. You can pray in tongues. Build yourself up!

But you, beloved, building yourselves up on your most holy faith, praying in the Holy Spirit, —Jude 1:20 NKJV

3. It Helps In Weakness.

In the same way, the Spirit helps us in our weakness. We do not know what we ought to pray for, but the Spirit himself intercedes for us with groans that words cannot express.
—Romans 8:26-27 NIV

The Spirit helps our weakness. The word weakness means: Infirmities (sickness) want of strength, weakness.

It also means to restrain from corrupt desires - To bear in trials and troubles.

Here's the implication in the Greek language:

> *The Holy Spirit takes hold together with you against your weakness. The Holy Spirit can help you not even to desire it anymore. Paul wrote, Now I would have you all speak with tongues,* —1 Corinthians 14:5 KJ21

Paul writes the Holy Spirit takes hold with us against our weakness. That's powerful, because we're not alone. The same Holy Spirit that worked in the lives of our heroes of the faith, like Peter and the disciples, is available to us. Take a moment at the end of the book to pray the powerful prayer so you can be baptized in the Holy Spirit. With the Holy Spirit's help, you have the power to be what God has called you to be. You can do what God says you can do. You will fulfill your purpose! You're strong, capable, empowered, and enabled to live in the deep. It is the life you were meant to live.

CHAPTER 11

ETERNITY

Peter's life was forever changed when he encountered Jesus on the shore that day. A decision to trust Jesus and launch out into the deep would just be the beginning. God's secret and unrevealed purposes for him would finally be discovered. The miraculous catch that Peter chose to abandon was insignificant compared to what his destiny would entail. Peter was invited to have a front-row seat to experience Jesus' ministry and miracles. After Jesus' death, Peter saw and encountered the risen Savior.

As the Holy Spirit stirred Peter's life, he overflowed with passion. He delivered a powerful and convicting message on the day of Pentecost that led to the salvation of three thousand people. Extraordinary! Millions of people would read Peter's sermon in the scriptures for generations to come. This is what "fishers of men" do, they cast a net with their lives to help save other people.

This is what "fishers of men" do: they cast a net with their lives to save other people.

Only Jesus can transform a fisherman into a phenomenal orator. Jesus can take a man who was mending his nets and use him to bring miracles into people's lives. Peter would not only walk on water, but as he walked along the road in Jerusalem, people would hope that his shadow would heal them.

> *More and more people believed in the Lord, and many men and women were added to the group of believers. So the people brought those who were sick into the streets and put them on little beds and mats. They were hoping that Peter's shadow might fall on them as he walked by. People came from all the towns around Jerusalem. They brought those who were sick or troubled by evil spirits. All of them were healed.*
> —Acts 5:14-16 ERV

Jesus can take a man who was mending his nets and use him to bring miracles into people's lives.

Remarkably, people would come from all the different towns around Jerusalem to see Peter and experience His miraculous ministry. Under the inspiration of the Holy Spirit, Peter wrote two books of the New Testament. His life was written about throughout the New Testament. It is estimated that billions of people have read the Bible over centuries. Scholars have spent their lives studying it, while rabbis, ministers, and priests have focused on interpreting, teaching, and preaching from its pages. Peter was not just an orator but an author in the best-selling book of all time.

Forever

Our actions here on earth will have eternal ramifications. When we close our eyes for the last time here on earth, in death, we will open them in heaven. As you walk the streets in heaven, the Scriptures tell us that on the wall of the beautiful city in heaven, we will see Peter's name and the names of the twelve apostles forever. Peter was called to have an eternal purpose. So are you!

And the wall of the city had twelve foundations [stones], and on them were the twelve names of the twelve apostles of the Lamb.
—Revelation 21:14 AMPC

God's Purposes for our life are eternal and will outlast our life here on earth.

The apostle Paul encourages us to live with eternity in mind, knowing that all we do for God's purposes will last.

For no other foundation can anyone lay than that which is already laid, which is Jesus Christ. 12 But if anyone builds on the foundation with gold, silver, precious stones, wood, hay, straw, 13 the work of each will become visible, for the Day will make it clear, because it will be revealed with fire, and the fire will test the quality of each one's work. 14 If what anyone has built survives, they will receive a reward. 15 If someone's work is burned up, they will suffer loss, but they themselves will be saved, but only as through fire.
—1 Corinthians 3:11-15 AMPC

Living for God and fulfilling His purpose for your life will have eternal rewards. Peter's life shows us that it's not how you start but how you finish that truly matters. I want my life to be driven by eternity.

I'm curious if Peter ever imagined his life would turn out so extraordinary. What God did in Peter, you couldn't just put in a five-year projection plan for your life. These are not the kind of things one would typically include on a vision board. I believe in goals and the power of vision and dreams. God uses visions often to motivate and inspire us. Don't limit God to just your dreams. God can exceed even your wildest dreams and blow your mind.

Now to Him Who, by (in consequence of) the [action of His] power that is at work within us, is able to [carry out His purpose and] do superabundantly, far over and above all that we [dare] ask or think [infinitely beyond our highest prayers, desires, thoughts, hopes, or dreams]
—Ephesians 3:20 AMPC

In the Amplified Classic Version Paul says God can do superabundantly, far above all that we can dare ask or think.

Today I dare you to take a step and defy the odds and think bigger, I dare you to tear the limits off. I dare you to stop making excuses. I dare you to pray big prayers, I dare you to make yourself available for God to use you. I dare you to pray for those that are sick, I dare you share your story with others. I dare you not to live an average live. I dare you to step out in faith today! You can launch into the deep because the power is already working in you.

Broken lives are waiting to be mended, and there are lost lives waiting to be found. The world is waiting for God's people to step into their purpose and live with power and passion.

> *For the creation waits with eager longing for the revealing of the children of God.* —Romans 8:19 NRSV

The time to launch is now! You can't wait any longer. Jesus is inviting you and calling you just as He did Peter. Peter wrote to us as he passes the baton to our generation.

> *But you are a chosen generation, a royal priesthood, a holy nation, His own special people, that you may proclaim the praises of Him who called you out of darkness into His marvelous light;* — 1 Peter 2:9 NKJV

The Passion translation reads,

> *But you are God's chosen treasure —priests who are kings, a spiritual "nation" set apart as God's devoted ones. He called you out of darkness to experience his marvelous light, and now he claims you as his very own. He did this so that you would broadcast his glorious wonders throughout the world.*
> 1 Peter 2:9 —TPT

God did this so that you would broadcast His glorious wonders throughout the world.

Eternity is in your heart! It's time for you to discover all the secret and unrevealed purposes God has for your life. This can only happen in the deep.

A POWERFUL PRAYER

Today, you can accept Jesus' invitation to be part of His family by becoming a child of God. You can be confident that one day, when you close your eyes for the last time on earth, you can open them in Heaven in the presence of God.

Pray this prayer loud, in faith, and say, Father God, thank you for sending your Son Jesus to die on the cross for me. Today, I realize your goodness and grace, and I repent. Forgive me of my sin. I turn away from sin and turn to you. Jesus, come into my heart. I receive your life in me. I confess to you, Jesus, as my Lord and Savior.

Baptize me today and fill me with your Holy Spirit, that I may speak with new tongues.

Lead me in the purposes that you have for my life. In Jesus' name, amen!

Now that you have been saved and filled with God's Holy Spirit, pray what God places on your heart. Open your mouth, and God will fill it with a heavenly language.

Congratulations! I want to be the first to welcome you to the family of God. Thank you for responding to God's abundant grace!

The Bible says in 2 Corinthians 5:17 "Therefore if anyone is in Christ, he is a new creation; old things have passed away; behold, all things have become new." —NKJV

Today you are new! I would encourage you to tell someone about the new decision you have made and attend a life-giving church that teaches God's Word. May you always remember how good God is. You are loved!

ABOUT THE AUTHOR

Phil Valdez is the founding senior pastor of Passion Life Church, a dynamic church in Murrieta, California. Phil is a graduate of Christ for the Nations Institute in Dallas, Texas. He has been helping and pastoring people for over thirty years.

Phil's desire is to help people discover their God-given purpose and release their full potential. With Phil's heartfelt and authentic communication style, he has been invited to speak at churches and conferences throughout the United States and abroad. Phil is married to his wife Valerie and has a son named Gavin.

For more information about this book and others that he has authored or to have Phil speak at your church or event, visit Philvaldez.org

For more information about Passion Life Church, visit

Passionlifechurch.com

Follow Phil on Instagram @PhilValdez and Facebook.

THANK YOU

Thank You to my Lord and Savior Jesus Christ for making this possible! You have given me a life beyond what I could have ever imagined.

To my wife Valerie, you are such a gem! You inspire me every day to be better. Your kind words always build me up. This book would not have been possible without you. I love you!

To my son Gavin, what a joy you are! You're the best kid ever! To see the Godly young man you are becoming makes me so proud! I love you!

To my Mom, Cathy Duncan, your Godly example has shaped my life. Your bold faith and love for God's Word is contagious. Thank you for always standing strong for our family!

Dan Duncan, thank you for your support and all your kind words. Your friendship to me has really meant the world.

To my sister Katie, and Jonathan, thank you for all your encouragement and advice with my projects. God has truly gifted you both. Thank you, Mendo Media for the beautiful Book cover design.

To my brother Jorge and Lily Valdez, thank you for all your advice and wisdom. You're not just family but great friends.

To the Perez family, you are friends that have become family. Inez, your prayers, support, and friendship have encouraged us more than you will ever know. Thank you, Grace Perez, for all the transcriptions you did to make this book happen.

To the great people of Passion Life Church, thank you for your prayers and commitment to the Lord. We Love You!

REFERENCES

Introduction:

New King James Bible – Copyright © 1982 by Thomas Nelson.

Wycliff Bible - CreateSpace Independent Publishing Platform

The Deer - https://heatonkent.com/

Chapter 1

New King James Bible – Copyright © 1982 by Thomas Nelson.

El Roi - https://www.biblestudytools.com/biblestudy/topicalstudies/reasons-to-praise-god-as-el-roi.html King James Version - @public domain

The Message Translation: NavPress; Authored by Eugene H. Peterson and published in segments from 1993 to 2002.

The Amplified Bible: produced jointly by Zondervan and The Lockman Foundation.

The Amplified Classic: The Lockman Foundation publishing.

Raining Fish – https://www.firstpost.com/explainers/raininghttps://www.firstpost.com/explainers/raining-fish-australian-town-lajamanu-fish-falling-from-the-skies-12198912.htmlfishaustralian-town-lajamanu-fish-falling-from-thehttps://www.firstpost.com/explainers/raining-fish-australian-town-lajamanu-fish-falling-from-the-skies-12198912.htmlskies12198912.html

Chapter 2

In "The Complete Word Study Dictionary" a Greek English dictionary edited by Spiros Zodhiates the word Deep is "Bathos" in Greek- Number 899

The Amplified Bible: produced jointly by Zondervan and The Lockman Foundation.

The Amplified Classic: The Lockman Foundation publishing.

Eternity - https://www.blueletterbible.org/lexicon/h5769/kjv/wlc/0-1/

Eternity 2 - https://www.blueletterbible.org/lexicon/h5956/kjv/wlc/0-1/

King James Version - @public domain

The Passion Translation - Broadstreet Publishing

Chapter 3

The American Psychological Association Article: https://www.apa.org/news/press/releases/stress/2022/concernedhttps://www.apa.org/news/press/releases/stress/2022/concerned-future-inflationfutureinflation#:~:text=More%20than%20three%2Dquart ers%2 0of,history%20that%20they%20can%20remember.

King James Version - @public domain

Lottery Winners - https://www.news4jax.com/features/2023/01/12/ripupthe-winning-ticket-5-reasons-why-winning-lotterycandestroy-lives/#:~:text=According%20to%20the%20National%20Endowment,of%20winners%20and%20their%20families

According to the National Endowment for Financial Education, 70% of lottery winners go bankrupt within a few years.

New King James Bible – Copyright © 1982 by Thomas Nelson.

The Amplified Classic: The Lockman Foundation publishing.

The Message Translation: NavPress; Authored by Eugene H. Peterson and published in segments from 1993 to 2002. "The Power Of Thank You – The Key to Finding Joy Again – Author Phil Valdez Publisher : BookBaby (December 30, 2020) ISBN-13 : 978-1098341701

New King James Bible – Copyright © 1982 by Thomas Nelson.

In "The Complete Word Study Dictionary" a Greek English dictionary edited by Spiros Zodhiates the word Repent is "Bathos" in Greek- Number 3339

New King James Bible – Copyright © 1982 by Thomas Nelson.

New King James Bible – Copyright © 1982 by Thomas Nelson.

New King James Bible – Copyright © 1982 by Thomas Nelson.

Make: https://www.blueletterbible.org/lexicon/g4160/kjv/tr/01/

Chapter 4

New King James Bible – Copyright © 1982 by Thomas Nelson.

New King James Bible – Copyright © 1982 by Thomas Nelson.

New King James Bible – Copyright © 1982 by Thomas Nelson.

Robert J. McKain Quote- https://www.proctorgallagherinstitute.com/26402/nowisyourtime#:~:text=Robert%20J.,time%20doing%20secon d%20t hings%20first.%E2%80%9D

The Amplified Classic: The Lockman Foundation publishing.

Csb Bible - https://csbible.com/

New King James Bible – Copyright © 1982 by Thomas Nelson.

New King James Bible – Copyright © 1982 by Thomas Nelson.

New King James Bible – Copyright © 1982 by Thomas Nelson.

John C. Maxwell Quote: https://www.servantleadershipinstitute.com/articles/2019/6/6/success-vs-significance#:~:text=John%20C.,significant%20people%20are%20always%20successful.%E2%80%9D

Chapter 5

King James Version - @public domain

Psychology Today - https://www.psychologytoday.com/us/blog/the-rightsidehttps://www.psychologytoday.com/us/blog/the-right-side-40/202206/how-avert-identity-crisis40/202206/how-avert-identity-crisis

New King James Bible – Copyright © 1982 by Thomas Nelson.

The Message Translation: NavPress; Authored by Eugene H. Peterson and published in segments from 1993 to 2002.

New King James Bible – Copyright © 1982 by Thomas Nelson.

New King James Bible – Copyright © 1982 by Thomas Nelson.

The Message Translation: NavPress; Authored by Eugene H. Peterson and published in segments from 1993 to 2002.

Reed - https://www.bible.com/reading-plans/28https://www.bible.com/reading-plans/28-joseph-prince/day/344josephprince/day/344

The Message Translation: NavPress; Authored by Eugene H. Peterson and published in segments from 1993 to 2002.

Chapter 6

The Amplified Classic: The Lockman Foundation publishing.

NIV- HarperCollins Christian Publishing, Inc.

New King James Bible – Copyright © 1982 by Thomas Nelson.

New King James Bible – Copyright © 1982 by Thomas Nelson.

The Amplified Bible: produced jointly by Zondervan and The Lockman Foundation.

New King James Bible – Copyright © 1982 by Thomas Nelson.

New King James Bible – Copyright © 1982 by Thomas Nelson.

New King James Bible – Copyright © 1982 by Thomas Nelson.

New King James Bible – Copyright © 1982 by Thomas Nelson.

NIV- HarperCollins Christian Publishing, Inc.

New King James Bible – Copyright © 1982 by Thomas Nelson.

The Amplified Classic: The Lockman Foundation publishing.

New King James Bible – Copyright © 1982 by Thomas Nelson.

New King James Bible – Copyright © 1982 by Thomas Nelson.

Passion: https://www.merriamwebster.com/dictionary/passion#:~:text=%3A%20a%20st rong%20liking%20or%20desire,a%20passion%20for%20o pera

New King James Bible – Copyright © 1982 by Thomas Nelson.

ASV Bible - The American Standard Version (ASV) – Public Domain

New King James Bible – Copyright © 1982 by Thomas Nelson.

The Passion Translation - Broadstreet Publishing Dr Miles

Monroe - https://www.munroeglobal.com/

Martin Luther king Jr Quote: https://www.goodreads.com/quotes/60289-no-one-reallyknows-why-they-are-alive-until-they

Chapter 7

New King James Bible – Copyright © 1982 by Thomas Nelson.

New King James Bible – Copyright © 1982 by Thomas Nelson.

New King James Bible – Copyright © 1982 by Thomas Nelson.

New King James Bible – Copyright © 1982 by Thomas Nelson.

NLT Bible – New Living Translation - Tyndale House Publishers

NIV- HarperCollins Christian Publishing, Inc.

The Amplified Classic: The Lockman Foundation publishing.

EHV- Evangelical Heritage Version - Northwestern Publishing House

National Science Foundation - https://www.stylist.co.uk/health/mentalhealth/psychology-negative-positive-thinkingtiktok/607424

Cornell University - https://www.cdaltonpsychology.com/blogrunningthoughts#:~:text=We%20can%20see%20that%20one,we%20worry%20about%20never%20happens.

New King James Bible – Copyright © 1982 by Thomas Nelson.

New King James Bible – Copyright © 1982 by Thomas Nelson.

New King James Bible – Copyright © 1982 by Thomas Nelson.

New King James Bible – Copyright © 1982 by Thomas Nelson.

Chapter 8

New King James Bible – Copyright © 1982 by Thomas Nelson.

ASV Bible - The American Standard Version (ASV) – Public Domain

ERV - Easy-to-Read Bible Version compiled by the World Bible Translation Center.

New King James Bible – Copyright © 1982 by Thomas Nelson.

New King James Bible – Copyright © 1982 by Thomas Nelson.

New King James Bible – Copyright © 1982 by Thomas Nelson.

Chapter 10

King James Version - @public domain King

James Version - @public domain

Paraklētos -
https://www.blueletterbible.org/lexicon/g3875/kjv/tr/01/

NIV- HarperCollins Christian Publishing, Inc.

New King James Bible – Copyright © 1982 by Thomas Nelson.

New King James Bible – Copyright © 1982 by Thomas Nelson.

"English Standard Version," Crossway publication

New King James Bible – Copyright © 1982 by Thomas Nelson.

Bill Johnson Quote - https://bjm.org/

New King James Bible – Copyright © 1982 by Thomas Nelson.

Kj21 - 21st Century King James Bible Publishers NIV-

HarperCollins Christian Publishing, Inc.

Chapter 11

ERV - Easy-to-Read Bible Version compiled by the World Bible Translation Center

The Amplified Classic: The Lockman Foundation publishing.

The Amplified Classic: The Lockman Foundation publishing.

NRSVA - New Revised Standard Version Updated Edition

A Powerful Prayer:

New King James Bible – Copyright © 1982 by Thomas Nelson.

Made in the USA
Monee, IL
22 September 2023

7527f09d-9323-4a40-b72a-b6fee759f171R01